Would You Marry You?

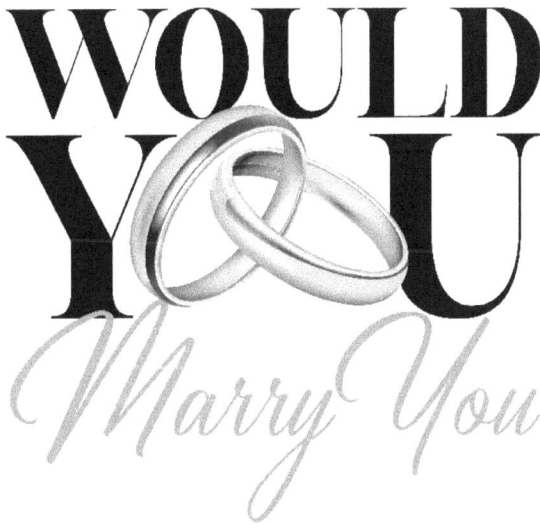

WOULD YOU

Marry You

TAFFINEY WILLIAMS

DEDICATION

To My Beloved Children,

LaQuanette, Malcolm, Adonte', and Brandi,

As I pen these words, my heart swells with gratitude and love for each of you. This book is not just a compilation of words on paper, but a testament to the incredible journey and profound impact relationships have had on our lives. Through the countless relationship ups and downs, you have stood by my side, offering unwavering love and support, teaching me the true meaning of family and resilience.

You are my greatest teachers and constant companions, witnessing the evolution of this movement from its humble beginnings to the transformative force it has become.

This dedication is a tribute to your unwavering faith in me and in the power of this message. It is a celebration of the bond we share, a bond forged not only by blood but by the shared experiences that have molded us into the individuals we are today.

May this book serve as a compass in your own lives, guiding you through the labyrinth of relationships and empowering you to embrace both the ups and downs with grace and understanding. May it remind you that the most profound relationship you will ever have is the one with yourself—a relationship built on self-love, acceptance, and growth.

My dear children, your presence in my life has been an immeasurable gift, and I am forever grateful for the privilege of being your Mom. Know that no matter where life takes you, my love and support will be an unwavering constant, a beacon of light to guide you through any storm.

With all my love, Mom

CONTENTS

ACKNOWLEDGMENTS

Writing this book has been a labor of love and a journey of self-discovery. It is with profound gratitude and joy that I take this moment to acknowledge those who have supported and inspired me throughout this process.

First and foremost, I want to express my heartfelt appreciation to God Almighty, the guiding force that led me on this journey of self-exploration. Through every twist and turn, He has provided me with the lessons and opportunities necessary to birth this movement.

I want to express my heartfelt appreciation to my children. You have been my pillars of strength, my motivation, and my most significant source of love and encouragement.

To my dear friends and family, thank you for standing by me. Your belief in my abilities and your presence in my life have been a constant reminder of the power of genuine connection.

I extend my deepest gratitude to my editor and the entire team for their dedication and expertise. Your insightful feedback has shaped this book into its best possible form.

To all the readers and supporters of "Would You Marry You," thank you for embracing this movement with open hearts and minds. Your enthusiasm for self-love and personal growth has been the driving force behind this endeavor, and I am deeply moved by your response.

I am also grateful to the countless individuals who trusted me to counsel, coach and mentor you. Sharing your personal life and experiences contributed to the rich tapestry of this book. Your bravery in opening up about your own relationship has made this work more authentic and relatable.

May all your relationships be enhanced by this growing movement.

WOULD YOU

Marry You

INTRO: Would You Marry You

What is marriage? It's a question that often stirs profound contemplation, and rightly so. Marriage stands as one of the most solemn covenants one can ever make, second only to their covenant with God. It is a sacred bond involving three individuals: God, one man, and one woman. Yet, in today's society, the true essence of marriage seems to have lost its significance, reduced to a mere temporary, feel-good, self-centered partnership, easily discarded when it fails to meet individual needs.

However, as we delve deeper into the word of God, we find that marriage is so much more. It is a reflection of the profound love that Christ shares with His church. Imagine, if you will, if Jesus had abandoned His believers when they disagreed with Him or failed to make Him happy. Thankfully, He didn't, and that serves as a reminder of the purpose behind marriage, as designed by God.

Marriage is not just about companionship; it goes beyond the surface and delves into spiritual growth and the beauty of intimacy. True intimacy, often defined as "into me see," encompasses a deliberate and profound connection with God, intertwining our spirits with those of our partners. This sacred bond becomes unbreakable, transcending time itself, encapsulating our past, present, and future.

Yet, true intimacy is not always easy to achieve. It requires courage, vulnerability, and a willingness to confront our flaws and imperfections. As we engage in intimate relationships with God and our significant others, we are bound to encounter uncomfortable truths about ourselves, unveiling aspects we might not even like.

But it is in this process that we discover the true essence of relationship readiness. Preparing for marriage illuminates our character flaws and spiritual challenges, making us realize how much we need to work on ourselves, shaping us into better versions of who we are meant to be. And this journey of self-discovery and growth is precisely what this book is all about.

So, let me ask you a few questions to ponder: Are you single, or are you just not married? There is a distinction between the two—being single means being free to give yourself to another without any strings or baggage attached. Do you truly know yourself? Your likes, dislikes, how you handle stress, and how you communicate your needs?

Furthermore, are you a good friend? Being teachable, humble, compassionate, and forgiving is crucial in building meaningful relationships. Do you understand your purpose in life and are you actively operating in it? Most importantly, do you love yourself? For you can only love another to the extent that you love yourself. Embracing your own company and finding joy in spending time with yourself is fundamental.

And let's not forget about stewardship—how are you managing your finances and taking care of your body? Your credit, employment status, and health are vital aspects of your life that require attention.

As you can see, there are many steps to take on the path of readiness before you can confidently answer the question, "Would You Marry You?" So, what if I'm already married? Well, this is for you as well. We are all on a Journey that we won't complete until we cross over into Glory so there is always room to grow. Now, if you arc ready to embark on this transformative journey of self-improvement and becoming the best version of yourself in this season, I invite you to claim God's truth as your own and align your heart with His, nurturing a firm foundation for your relationships.

Welcome to the Journey!

WOULD YOU

Marry You

Preface: My Journey from C.O.L.D to H.O.T.

What was it about me that kept leading me down the same path, attracting the same kind of men? Each relationship seemed different on the surface, but the recurring challenge of infidelity haunted me. Two failed marriages behind me and the possibility of a third on the horizon, I could not help but realize that the common denominator in every relationship was me. It was a tough pill to swallow, but I had to acknowledge that some of my relationship struggles were perpetuated by my own actions and beliefs.

With every failed marriage, the lies I held about myself became more apparent, and I found myself at a crossroads – either give up or try again. It felt like I was going insane, doing the same thing but expecting different results. It was then that I had a moment of clarity: If I didn't change anything about myself, nothing would change in my relationships either. I couldn't control the other person, but I could control myself, and I was determined to enter any future covenant with a healed heart, a renewed mind, and the heart of the King I served.

I found myself in the "in-between" – not married, but not truly single either. I was caught in the clutches of my past, closed off to love and deliverance, making me C.O.L.D. I knew I needed healing before I could be found again, and that's when a hard question confronted me – "Would You Even Marry You?" To answer truthfully, I had to get H.O.T – Honest, Open, and Transparent. I needed to look beyond fleeting emotions and commit to emotional honesty, refusing to be a prisoner of my feelings any longer.

When I finally opened my heart to God, questions flooded my mind. Was I truly the "good thing" that someone would find? Could I love unconditionally like Christ without expecting anything in return? Would I make the same mistakes again? In the midst of these questions, God gently reminded me to stop striving and trust in Him. He was creating something new in me. As I sought His will, I realized I could be anxious for nothing, as His peace would guard my heart and mind.

The journey towards transformation led me to repentance, where I found the truth of my identity in Christ. I discovered that my salvation was justified by grace through faith, and I belonged to the King. My trust shifted from relying on others to depending on my Heavenly Father, who loved me unconditionally. Trials were not meant to hurt me but to prepare me for the calling He had placed on my life – including the ministry of marriage, serving selflessly as Christ did.

As I peeled back the layers of wounds that had closed before healing properly, I learned to unlearn the lies and break agreements with my old self. The journey was challenging, but I embraced it with a Romans 8:28 understanding, choosing joy daily as my heart healed and my mind renewed. God lovingly "peeled the layers" to get me closer to the core, where growth and reproduction could take place.

Now, I invite you to join me on this transformative journey, to get H.O.T. – Honest, Open, and Transparent. Are you ready to become that good thing and experience the love God has in store for you? It's time to embrace the journey and discover the depths of love, acceptance, and healing that await you. Welcome to your path from C.O.L.D to H.O.T!

I WEAR A MASK

Do not be fooled by me, don't be fooled by the face you see, I wear a mask.

I wear one thousand masks, mask that I'm afraid to take off and none of them are really me.

Pretending is an art that is second nature to me, but do not be fooled.

I give the impression that I am secure, that I am good, that all is sunny and unruffled within me, that confidence is my game, that the water is calm, that I am in command

and that I need no one.

But do not believe me, please don't believe me.

My surface may seem smooth, but my surface is a mask, my ever-changing mask.

Beneath it lies no compliance, beneath it dwells the real me, in confusion, in shame, in loneliness. Fearing that if they only knew the real me, I would not be accepted. So, I hide that.

I do not want anybody to know that I dance in the mirror or that my favorite hairstyles from the 80s.

I panic at the thought of my weakness and insecurities being exposed.

That is why I frantically create a mask to hide behind, a nonchalant sophisticated façade' to help me pretend. To shield me from the glance and knows. But such a glance is my Salvation and I know it.

I have worn a mask for so long I don't remember everything about who I really AM. I am lost in the middle of a crowd, I'm silent even when I'm talking, and I'm blind with my eyes wide open.

I wear a mask. Who can get to know me when I don't even know myself, can't help but be alone in a room full of friends that only know the mask I wear?

How can others accept me, when I haven't accepted myself?

Do they love me, or do they love my mask?

Do I love me, or do I love my mask?

Do I even know what love is? It is the only thing that can free me from myself from the lies that I have to hide behind the mask to feel that I am really something.

Who am I, you might wonder?

I am most men you meet, I'm most women you meet, I'm right in front of you, please, just love me. Even if it is the me you can't see.

WOULD YOU
Marry You

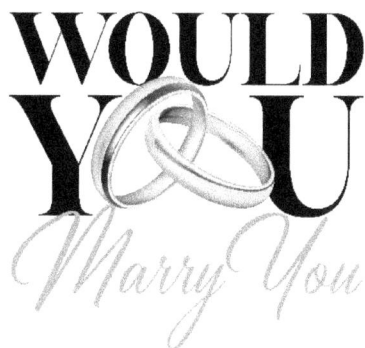

Chapter 1: Remove the MASK- Become Authentically You

Many years ago, I stumbled upon a simple yet profound question: "Who are you?" My initial response seemed straightforward – a mother, a wife, a teacher – the roles that defined me. But then came the unexpected twist – if these roles were stripped away, would I still be me? This revelation set my mind spinning, shedding light on the struggles many women face, from empty nest syndrome to identity crises when career paths shift. The core of the issue lies in allowing our positions and titles to define us, leaving us feeling inadequate, unimportant, or lost when those roles change.

As I processed this revelation, my mind underwent a transformation. I began to understand why challenging seasons, unforeseen incidents, and unwelcome situations seemed to trap me under the weight of trauma. It was because I had allowed my identity to be tethered to external circumstances. Perhaps you can relate to this as well – if so, let's give each other an air "high five."

During the tumultuous time of a pending divorce when my identity as a "wife" was threatened, I felt abandoned, insecure, unprotected, and deeply depressed. I questioned my worth and blamed myself for my husband's unfaithfulness and eventual abandonment of our marriage. In the midst of my despair, the Lord reminded me that He had the final say.

The truth is, God is crystal clear about who we are. Once we accept our relationship with Him, we become His children, seated in Heavenly places with Christ Jesus. We are a chosen people, a royal priesthood, and we inherit the promises of our Father God. But all too often, we resonate more with what others say about us than with what God declares. We allow our experiences, titles, and positions to dictate our identity, causing our world to crumble when circumstances are beyond our control. However, God's Word assures us that all things work together for our good, and He fearfully and wonderfully created each of us. He knows the plans He has for us, and He knew us before we were even formed in our mother's womb.

So, let us consider this truth: If God knew us before our conception, can any event or circumstance change who we are to Him? Can a breakup, divorce, strained friendship, job loss, molestation, time spent in jail, addiction, bullying, or hurtful words from family alter our identity in His eyes? Whose truth will we choose to believe?

In this journey of embracing our imperfections, we must recognize that human uniqueness adds spice to life. We are all different in millions of ways, and some of these differences may seem like imperfections, leaving us feeling self-conscious, ashamed, and guilty. But learning to embrace these differences and accepting ourselves wholly is essential to living a fulfilling life. It takes time and practice, but with effort, we can learn to be our authentic selves by accepting and celebrating what makes us unique.

Part of this process involves acknowledging that we cannot always control everything in our lives. Setting goals to change and improve is commendable, but there are certain aspects of ourselves that we simply cannot alter. Instead of striving for the impossible, we must embrace the freedom of letting go and accepting ourselves, imperfections and all. Our ability to change comes through the love of God operating in and through us.

Additionally, we must remember that no one on this planet is perfect. We all make mistakes and possess flaws or aspects of ourselves that we may dislike. Rather than feeling isolated due to our imperfections, we should remind ourselves that we are not alone in these struggles. Many others share similar feelings and experiences and knowing that we are part of a community who can understand and empathize with us can be a source of comfort.

But what often hinders us from embracing our true selves is the masks we wear. At times, even those deeply connected to their authentic selves feel compelled to put on a facade. These masks are employed in various situations to hide our true selves from others. Whether it's the people pleaser, the in-crowder, the denier, the dampener, or the shy mask, they all serve to conceal our true identity.

However, the journey to freedom starts with removing the mask and actively choosing not to compare ourselves to others. Comparison is indeed the thief of joy, leading us to envy the seemingly perfect lives of others. We must recognize that everyone has their struggles, and what we see on social media is often a highlight reel, not the full picture. When we stop comparing and start embracing our imperfections, we can focus on our happiness and authenticity, unapologetically being ourselves – the unique beings God created us to be.

So, I invite you to embark on this journey of self-discovery and acceptance, removing the masks that have concealed your true self for far too long. Embrace your imperfections, celebrate your uniqueness, and let the love of God shine through you. By doing so, you will find freedom, joy, and a deeper connection to the truth of who you are – fearfully and wonderfully made by the Creator Himself. It's time to remove the mask and step into the fullness of your authentic self.

Mask 1: The People Pleaser - (Orphan Spirit)

The people pleasing mask is worn when someone has a hard time saying no. Perhaps they feel extreme guilt when they have to tell somebody no or feel like they must always say yes in order to win favor with someone, but regardless of the reason, the people pleaser mask is a common one used to cover the true self. If you're focused on making other people happy constantly, there's a great chance that you aren't listening to your true self.

Mask 2: The In-Crowder – (Orphan Spirit)

People who wear the in-crowd mask are similar to the people pleasers, but they differ in one important way: They do not want to lose favor with a specific person or group of people.

Humans, like many other creatures, have a herd mentality. There's safety in numbers; when you find a group of like-minded folks, you can feel a sense of relief and belonging. However, if the group's expectations cause you to hide your true self, you're using that in-crowder mask to do yourself more harm than good.

Mask 3: The Denier – (Orphan Spirit)

Self-doubt and denial are the worst–it can be super tough to come to terms with who you truly are. If you find yourself fighting against your true self, you may be wearing the mask of the denier.

Unlike denying yourself for the sake of others' happiness, you're denying your true self compassion, acceptance, and respect. In this case, you may not be wearing the denier mask for others; instead, you're wearing it for yourself. Rather than accepting yourself for who you are, you may try forcing yourself into something that goes against who you truly are.

Mask 4: The Dampener

Wearing the mask of the dampener results in a silencing of the true self. Someone who puts the dampener mask over their true self may feel like their personalities are too strong or overbearing, thus making them unappealing to new people.

Rather than allowing your true self to be revealed to others, you may dampen your personality, actions, or words (shrink) in an effort to seem more likeable or approachable. Rather than being your true, honest self, you keep the dampener mask on because you think your true self might be "too much" for other people to handle.

Mask 5: The Shy

Meeting new people and getting acclimated to a new group is tough; many people may call on the mask of the shy at different points in their lives. The mask of the shy is similar to the dampener, but it has one key difference: People who pull out the mask of the shy may feel afraid or intimidated themselves.

Exposing your true self to new people, especially early on in a new relationship with them, feels raw and vulnerable. Rather than going full steam ahead with your true self, you may choose to cover it with the mask of the shy first by choosing words carefully, acting differently, and learning intently about the new people before making any true self-directed actions.

WOULD Y U Marry You

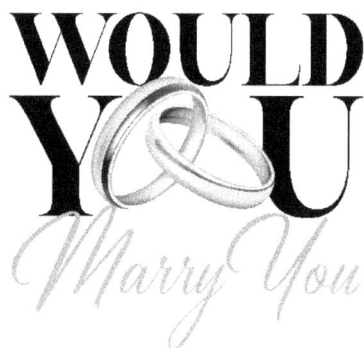

Chapter 2: Unraveling Soul Ties and Healing Soul Hurts

In the depths of the human soul lies a labyrinth of interconnected thoughts, emotions, and actions. The tripartite nature of the soul – mind, emotions, and will – gives rise to a fascinating dynamic where a thought, when allowed to linger, sparks an emotion, which in turn influences our actions. This intricate interplay is at the heart of the concept of "soul ties."

To comprehend the profound implications of soul ties, one must understand the three elements that constitute the soul. The mind, the repository of our thoughts, is where seeds of ideas are planted and where they take root if given the opportunity. Emotions, the expressive aspect of the soul, are the natural outcome of our thoughts, leading to feelings of joy, sorrow, anger, or love. Finally, the will is the governing power over our actions, responding to the thoughts and emotions that have taken hold in the mind.

Soul ties emerge when thoughts are allowed to linger and give birth to emotions, inevitably influencing our actions and shaping our choices. These ties can exert both moral and legal obligations over us, becoming restraining powers, influential forces, or even binding duties. Understanding the intricacies of soul ties is crucial for identifying their positive and negative manifestations in our lives.

While soul ties are often associated with physical intimacy, they go beyond mere sexual connections. Any thought, whether from a parent, friend, spouse, or any individual, that takes residence in our minds and evokes emotions affecting our behavior constitutes a soul tie. These relational connections can be both godly and ungodly, shaping the core of our beliefs, actions, and attitudes.

The concept of soul ties is not confined to specific relationships or scenarios. In fact, they manifest in various ways, influencing how we interact with God, others, and ourselves. Understanding the diverse forms of soul ties is essential for unraveling the complex web they weave in our lives.

A godly soul tie is the connection we share with God Himself. This divine bond draws us closer to His love, compassion, grace, and forgiveness. When we contemplate thoughts that mirror His goodness, joy, and peace, we experience emotions that reflect these attributes, and our actions align with the character of our Heavenly Father. This is the ideal soul tie that all believers should strive to nurture.

However, ungodly soul ties can be insidious, leading us down paths of dysfunction and negative behavioral patterns. Often stemming from generational influences or traumatic experiences, these soul ties become deeply ingrained, affecting our beliefs about ourselves and the world around us. Until we renew our minds to the heart of God, we may remain unaware of how these ungodly ties create emotions and behaviors that do not align with His character.

Family dynamics and upbringing play a significant role in the formation of ungodly soul ties. Our perception of love, acceptance, and worthiness is shaped during our formative years. If we experience rejection, neglect, or abuse, it can lead to ungodly soul ties that entangle our identities and influence how we relate to others.

Breaking free from these ungodly soul ties requires intentional effort and a willingness to renew our minds continuously. As we realign our thoughts and emotions with God's truth, we break the chains that have bound us to negative patterns and belief systems. This process empowers us to step into our true identity as beloved children of God, free from the bondage of past hurts and destructive soul ties.

Romantic relationships hold a unique place in the realm of soul ties. Sexuality, being a holistic experience that involves the body, soul, and spirit, goes beyond mere physical intimacy. It forges profound emotional connections, leading to what is known as "limbic bonding." Usually the woman, to form deeper attachments and experience hurt when the affair ends because the limbic portion of the brain is larger in women than it is in men.

The biblical perspective on sexual intimacy speaks to the union of two individuals, making them one flesh. This spiritual and emotional binding creates a covenant of marriage. Thus, the question arises: Are we genuinely single, or are we merely not married? How much of our past sexual encounters do we carry into our marriages, and are we truly free to give ourselves wholly to our spouse?

In contemporary society, the idea of casual sexual encounters has become prevalent, often leading to the misinterpretation of soul ties. Dr. Daniel Amen, in his book "Change Your Brain, Change Your Life," explains that neurochemical changes occur during sexual intimacy, leading to limbic bonding. This bonding fosters emotional connections between individuals, even in seemingly casual affairs.

The consequences of romantic soul ties can be profound, impacting individuals long after a relationship ends. The lingering thoughts and emotions about a previous partner can influence subsequent marital unions, leaving one or both parties feeling unfulfilled and unable to fully commit to their spouse.

Adultery exemplifies the depth of romantic soul ties and their impact on marital relationships. Emotional and spiritual bonds form with someone outside the marriage, diluting the commitment to the covenant with one's spouse. The lingering thoughts and emotions about the other person can continue even after the affair ends, leaving individuals feeling torn and conflicted.

Breaking free from romantic soul ties necessitates repentance, a change of mind, and a conscious decision to disentangle ourselves from past emotional connections. It requires a deep renewal of the mind and a realignment with God's truth about love, commitment, and intimacy. Only then can we experience the freedom to love our spouses without conditions and build thriving, healthy marriages.

Soul hurts, deeply rooted in disappointment, shame, and guilt, are among the most challenging wounds to heal from. The feeling of unworthiness that seeps into every cell of our bodies can be overwhelming, affecting our emotional and physical well-being. Soul hurts have far-reaching effects, creating a ripple effect that transcends generations, impacting our children and future descendants.

The pain from soul hurts is akin to a deep bruise that we tend to protect or overcompensate for. We may erect walls to shield ourselves from further pain, unintentionally sabotaging our own happiness and intimacy with others. In doing so, we may become emotionally detached, rude, or numb, seeking to avoid vulnerability.

Healing from soul hurts requires a courageous approach, akin to treating an infected wound. Just as we must cut open a wound, cleanse it, and allow it to heal from the inside out, we must face the pain head-on and bring it before Jesus for deliverance. Like delivering a package to a recipient, we must deliver our pain to Jesus, allowing Him to transform us from the inside out.

One critical aspect of healing from soul hurts is understanding the impact of past experiences on our ability to receive and give love. When we have experienced rejection or conditional love from others, we may unwittingly place limitations or conditions on God's love for us. These self-imposed barriers hinder our ability to experience the fullness of God's unconditional love.

Breaking down these emotional walls allows us to experience God's love at a deeper level, tearing down the barriers that have kept Him at a distance. This transformative journey allows us to embrace the feminine character of God through the Holy Spirit, experiencing His compassion, grace, and comfort as we lay our heads on His chest and find solace in His presence.

Soul hurts often lead to a need for protection, resulting in walls that hinder intimacy and connection with others. Childhood experiences, such as feeling unimportant or rejected by our parents, sow seeds of abandonment, guilt, and shame that take root and grow into trees, impacting every relationship we engage in.

To experience true healing, we must be willing to confront these soul hurts, tear down the walls, and allow ourselves to be vulnerable once more. As we face our pain with Jesus at our side, we can experience a love that transcends human limitations, allowing us to love ourselves and others unconditionally.

Breaking free from soul ties and healing from soul hurts is a transformative process that leads to freedom and wholeness. This journey requires courage, vulnerability, and a willingness to trust God with our deepest wounds and insecurities. As we navigate this path, we will discover the liberating power of God's love and grace, bringing transformation to every area of our lives.

The first step in breaking free from soul ties and soul hurts is recognizing their existence and impact. Identifying ungodly soul ties and acknowledging their hold on our thoughts and emotions empowers us to confront them head-on. Likewise, acknowledging the presence of soul hurts and their influence on our relationships enables us to address the deep-rooted wounds that hinder our emotional and spiritual growth.

Repentance, the act of changing our minds and coming out of agreement with ungodly attachments, is essential in breaking free from soul ties. The process of renewing our minds continuously involves replacing negative thought patterns with God's truth and aligning our will with His perfect will. Through this ongoing transformation, we can begin to break the chains that have bound us to ungodly patterns.

Breaking free from romantic soul ties requires intentional choices to cut emotional and spiritual bonds with past partners. Repentance, coupled with a desire to embrace God's design for sexuality and intimacy, allows us to experience healing and restoration in our marital relationships. This newfound freedom enables us to love our spouses without comparison or emotional baggage, creating a foundation of trust and intimacy.

To heal from soul hurts, we must be brave enough to face our pain and allow Jesus to work in our lives. Letting go of self-imposed barriers and embracing vulnerability allows us to experience the depths of God's love and acceptance. As we bring our pain before Him, He replaces our shame with worthiness, our guilt with forgiveness, and our disappointment with hope.

Embracing our identity as beloved children of God empowers us to tear down the walls, we have erected in an attempt to protect ourselves. We can love others unconditionally, extending grace and compassion to those around us. The freedom found in God's love enables us to build authentic and intimate relationships, free from the limitations of soul ties and soul hurts.

Conclusion: Embrace Your Journey to Wholeness

Breaking up with bondage involves a journey of self-discovery, healing, and transformation. The complexities of soul ties and soul hurts can be overwhelming, but the freedom and wholeness that await us make the journey worth every step.

By identifying and breaking free from ungodly soul ties, we release ourselves from negative thought patterns and emotional baggage. Likewise, healing from soul hurts enables us to tear down emotional walls and embrace vulnerability, allowing us to experience God's love and extend it to others.

This transformative journey empowers us to embrace our true identity as beloved children of God, free from the chains of bondage that have hindered our growth and relationships. As we walk in the fullness of God's love, grace, and forgiveness, we become vessels of healing and hope to those around us.

Remember, you are fearfully and wonderfully created by a God who loves you unconditionally. Embrace your imperfections, for they are part of the unique masterpiece that God has designed. Trust in His plan for your life and let go of the soul ties and soul hurts that have held you captive. Embrace your journey to wholeness, for it is in the breaking up with bondage that you will find true freedom and abundant life.

Dear Heavenly Father, I thank You for giving me access to Your word that I may intentionally renew my mind. Lord, I confess that I have allowed thoughts of people and things from my past to affect my emotions. I have acted out of emotions and preconceived expectations of rejection, abandonment, and fear. Please bring to mind every person that I have an unhealthy soultie to so that I can break it now. In Jesus' name I pray. Amen

Breaking soul-ties is very important. Now make a list of everyone that you have had any sexual connections with. Whether consensual (masturbation, intercourse, etc.) or nonconsensual (molestation, rape, etc.) or even if it was in your mind (fantasy, pornography, etc.). Any sexual sin. These sexual bondages need to be broken. Most married people forget to add their spouse if there was activity prior to their marriage. Also add anyone that has any influence over your decisions.

Lord Jesus, I ask You to break the Ungodly soul-tie with

_____ spiritually, physically, mentally and

emotionally. Amen, I renounce any use of my body as an

instrument of unrighteousness in sexual sin. I ask You to

cleanse me. I choose to present my body as a living

sacrifice and choose to keep it holy from this day

forward. I reserve the sexual use of my body for marriage

and reject the lie that my body is unclean or dirty as a

result of my past sexual experiences because You Lord

have forgiven me and made me whole. In Jesus name.

Amen

Dear Heavenly Father, I thank You for never leaving me even when things were not going well. I ask for you to continue with me as I allow myself to be honest and vulnerable to recall the traumatic events that have hurt me. Lord, I know You don't desire for me to carry past hurts into the plans you have for my future. Please prepare me to revisit these events with the understanding that this deliverance will set my thoughts, emotions, and actions in the direction you desire for me. Lord, I confess that I have treated myself and others in ways that were based on soul hurt and allowed that pain to dictate my expectations of others. Please bring to mind all the places that trauma has been allowed to enter and affect my mind, emotions, and will. In Jesus' name I pray. Amen

Make note of each negative impact or emotion. The people involved, the location, and every thought that ran through your mind at that time. How this event made you feel is very important as well. This will require you to be vulnerable. Getting H.O.T. is not easy, however it's the only way to healing and wholeness. Honesty with God, and yourself. Is the first step. Whether you thought about killing someone, or you hated yourself for falling for the same trick, write it down so you can deal with it in a later step. Look over all that you have written and identify cycles, behaviors leading up to events, habits, and challenges.

Action: Imagine every event individually and slice it up like a pie, imagine Jesus, our intercessor, standing in front of you, and deliver every emotion, thought, and habit to him. Even if it includes anger or disappointment with God. It's time to get your voice back from underneath the trauma. Get Un-Trapped. When a package is delivered it changes ownership from the person delivering it to the person it's being delivered to. Deliver it to Jesus.

For every painful memory that God reveals on your list, pray aloud:

Lord Jesus, I choose to deliver to you the pain of {name the trauma} because it made me feel {share the feelings; fear, anger, worthless, etc.}. Lord, I choose to walk from under the cloud of pain caused by trauma and into the sunshine of Your healing, grace, and mercy. I declare that I am wonderfully made in Your image, and I am who You say that I am. I break every cycle, and ungodly thought, behavior, and habit I walked in agreement with based on these events and ask You to heal my damaged emotions. Create a clean heart in me, renew my spirit, and give me a hunger and thirst to renew my mind. Thank You for setting me free from the trap of past trauma. I now ask You to bless those who have hurt me. In Jesus' name, I pray. Amen

Chapter 3: Parental Issues - The Impact on Our Lives

Childhood experiences within our homes have a profound influence on shaping our adult lives. The financial, relational, and spiritual norms established during our formative years become the lens through which we perceive and experience the world. Our brains absorb and process the information made available to us, guiding us accordingly in our interactions and decision-making. Consequently, the effects of these experiences can lead to dysfunction in various aspects of our lives, impacting our relationships, beliefs, and emotional well-being. When it comes to understanding the roots of these challenges and issues, much can be traced back to our fathers, making it essential to address the concept of "daddy issues."

"Train up a child in the way he should go; even when he is old, he will not depart from it." (Proverbs 22:6) This biblical verse highlights the critical role fathers play in the lives of their children. Let us explore the significance of fathers and their impact on shaping our development.

Fathers are intended to be spiritual leaders within their families. They are responsible for guiding and modeling faith in the household, particularly in the case of boys. A father's influence in spiritual matters can significantly shape the faith and values of their children, leaving a lasting impact on their spiritual journey.

Fathers play a crucial role in validating their children's existence and purpose. They have a profound influence on shaping their children's identity, sense of purpose, and significance in the world. When children receive affirmation and support from their fathers, it fosters a healthy self-esteem and a positive outlook on life.

Fathers provide a strong masculine presence that instills a sense of safety and security in their children. This protection extends beyond physical safety and encompasses emotional and psychological well-being. A father's presence helps children navigate the world with confidence, knowing they are not vulnerable to negative external forces.

A father's influence contributes to shaping a child's sexual identity and understanding of gender roles in interpersonal relationships. This influence helps children develop a clear understanding of masculinity, femininity, and the differences between the roles of men and women in society.

Fathers often foster a balanced life approach that is not overly driven by emotions. They bring a logical and practical perspective to decision-making, helping their children see situations from a more objective standpoint.

Fathers serve as a counterbalance to the nurturing and compassionate nature of motherly figures. They provide authoritative guidance and set boundaries, helping children develop a sense of responsibility and accountability through discipline.

While mothers play an equally significant role in a child's life, fathers and mothers contribute distinct qualities to their children's development. The unique contributions of both parents create a balance that nurtures the emotional and psychological growth of their children.

Mothers, being the first caregivers from the moment of pregnancy and throughout a child's early years, form strong emotional bonds with their children. The way mothers interact during these crucial stages leaves a deep impact on a child's social and emotional development in later years.

Here are some of the significant roles mothers play in a child's life:

Mothers are often the first ones to connect with their children, fostering strong emotional bonds during pregnancy and infancy. The early interactions and care provided by mothers significantly influence a child's social and emotional development.

Mothers are responsible for providing a nurturing and supportive environment that encourages movement, creativity, and play. This setting fosters proper development and growth during a child's formative years.

Mothers play a vital role in teaching their children to trust and be trustworthy. Their kindness, love, and care serve as models for children to emulate as they mature, leading them to develop secure and confident emotional foundations.

Mothers reinforce the importance of family bonds and unity by encouraging family meals and quality time spent together. They often serve as the backbone that holds the family together, promoting a sense of belonging and support within the family unit.

Mothers understand and respond to their children's thoughts and emotions, teaching them empathy and the ability to understand other people's perspectives. This sensitivity fosters healthy relationships and emotional intelligence as children grow into adults.

A mother's nurturing and caring nature instills a positive attitude in children. Her support during challenging times teaches them that life can be handled in a better way, no matter the difficulties they may face.

Unfortunately, the absence of active parents can lead to relational dysfunction, resulting in children being more likely to engage in behaviors such as having children outside of marriage or experiencing divorce. Furthermore, females may be more susceptible to exploitation by men due to their hindered development in handling aggression and responding to challenging situations.

The separation from our Heavenly Father since the fall of

man in the Garden of Eden has led to a sense of not belonging and seeking acceptance, security, and significance elsewhere. The consequences of this earthly separation can lead to chaos, narcissism, and people-pleasing tendencies as we try to fill the God-sized hole in our hearts.

However, there is hope for healing and restoration. Here are some steps to find healing from parental issues:

1. Forgiveness:

Take the time to genuinely forgive your parents individually for their absence or any impact their presence may have had on your life. Allow the love of God to guide you to find peace with your parents, fostering a spirit of forgiveness.

2. Change Your Belief System:

Our lives cannot outpace our thoughts. Evaluate your thoughts and beliefs about yourself as a result of having an absent or dysfunctional parent. Challenge and replace negative thought patterns with positive, affirming beliefs.

3. Embrace Your Heavenly Father:

Allow God to be your true Father and guide your life. Embrace His word, love, guidance, and wisdom, finding the affirmation and protection you need in His presence.

4. Acknowledge the Divine Plan:

Acknowledge the divine plan that protected you from a

toxic or counterproductive parental relationship. Celebrate the ways in which your experiences have contributed to your life's character and growth.

5. Seek Healthy Mechanisms for Growth:

Develop areas of weakness through mentorship, seeking guidance from spiritual parents, reading, or engaging in constructive conversations. Commit to creating positive shifts in the dynamic of parenting within your community.

Breaking free from parental issues involves a process of healing and transformation. By embracing forgiveness, changing our belief systems, and seeking God as our true Father, we can experience healing and wholeness in our lives. As we release the chains of our past and embrace the love and affirmation of our Heavenly Father, we find freedom from chaos, narcissism, and the need to seek validation elsewhere. Let us journey together toward healing and restoration as we open our hearts to the transformative power of love and forgiveness.

Dear Heavenly Father, I thank You for Your patience when I hurt You by behaving in a way that did not honor You and the gift of Your son Jesus. Lord, I know that Your kindness and gift of the Holy Spirit has led me to repentance (Romans 2:4). I confess that I have not extended that same kindness, and patience toward my parents who were not there for me, hurt and or offended me. Instead, I have held onto anger, bitterness, and resentment toward them for their deficiency and allowed the pain to dictate my expectations of them and others. I choose now to let go and forgive them from my heart. Thank you for the gift of forgiveness. In Jesus' name I pray. Amen

WOULD YOU

Marry You

Chapter 4: Love Without Limits or Conditions

As I sat at my dining table, having a deep conversation with my Father God, His question struck me like a bolt of lightning. "Have you placed conditions on my love based on the love you've experienced from humans?" His words pierced my heart, and I found myself reflecting on the walls I had built to protect myself from hurt and rejection. But in doing so, I had unknowingly kept God out as well. I realized that my ability to love others unconditionally stemmed from experiencing God's love and embracing my identity as His beloved child.

This journey towards experiencing God's love without conditions became my passion. I knew I needed to tear down the walls that had separated me from His unconditional love and embrace the feminine character of God through the Holy Spirit's power. It was in His embrace that I found compassion, grace, and comfort, allowing myself to be vulnerable, weak, naked, and unashamed.

Life throws various experiences our way, leading us to build walls around our hearts as protection. But those walls end up doing more harm than good. The enemy uses them to plant seeds of lies, like feelings of abandonment, guilt, and shame. These seeds take root, bearing fruit that negatively affects every relationship we engage in.

Yet, God desires for us to tear down these walls and experience His love in its purest form. Love, as God defines it, is an unselfish expression of servitude. It's a word that's both overused and underappreciated in human interactions. Love, as God embodies it, is kind, patient, and forgiving. Without God, there can be no true love. When we experience God's love, we are empowered to love ourselves and others unconditionally.

To tear down these walls hindering our experience of God's love, we must take several steps:

First, we must realize the lies we've believed about ourselves based on our past experiences and relationships. Distinguishing between the facts of a situation and the truth God reveals to us allows us to replace those lies with His truth.

Secondly, submitting to God is not about being undervalued or insignificant; it's about finding safety, protection, and concern in His love. Surrendering to God's will allows us to experience His unconditional love fully.

Walking in God's truth is essential. Our emotions and perceptions can often lead us astray. But by walking in His truth, we can overcome negative emotions and embrace love without conditions.

Experiencing love without conditions starts with understanding the lies we've believed about ourselves based on our past experiences and relationships. Through prayer and introspection, we can allow God to reveal His truth to us and understand our true identity in Him. Recognizing the cycles of insanity in our lives and breaking free from negative patterns becomes possible as we tear down the walls and embrace God's love.

LOVE An unspoken expression of servitude. A four-letter word that denotes complete care, compassion, and cultivation of the gifts in a person which can only come from God. The most over-used yet least understood word amongst humans. Love. God is Love. Love is kind, love is patient and doesn't hold on to wrong. No God, no love. The unselfish act of giving your life for your brother. See if you don't know the love of God You can't love another. Love, choosing to do whatever it takes to help a person become the best version of themselves. Love God, Love Yourself, then and only then can you love others.

Have you ever "felt some kind of way" because a friend walked past and didn't speak? Did you stop and think: Maybe she's looking for someone. Maybe he got a disturbing phone call before he got here. Maybe their child didn't come home last night. Do you remember times when your mind was far away from where your body was? The facts were just that, facts. But the truth is far from what the facts show.

So many things that cause us to erect walls in life. To allow seeds of negative emotions to take root in our lives. We see God through these blurry lenses. The only way to experience this true authentic level of love is through a personal relationship with the Savior of our souls. To do so, we must tear down this wall of lies and embrace the truth of God.

1.What lies have you believed about yourself and adopted as your identity based on the circumstances of your birth, family you were born into and your experiences before age 5?

2. What lies have you believed about yourself as a result of the relationship with the father figure in your life?

3. What lies have you believed about yourself based on illnesses, accidents, and family addictions?

4. What lies have you believed based on losses in your life? Whether through death, loss of a job or loss of a relationship?

5. What lies have you believed about yourself based on your first exposure to sexual conversation or encounter?

6. What lies have you believed based on others' emotions or acceptance of you?

7. What lies have you believed based on not feeling loved by those you felt should know how to love you?

8. Pray and ask God to reveal His truth to you about your identity.

9. What are the lessons God would have you learn?

10. What are the cycles of insanity in my life?

11. Father God what lies have I OWNED because of them?

12. What seeds have been watered or have taken root in my life?

13. What do you say about me Lord?

In conclusion, love without conditions is an invitation from God to experience His true love, free from the walls we've built around our hearts. As we tear down these walls and embrace His unconditional love, we find healing and restoration. We can love ourselves and others authentically and without reservation. Love, in its purest form, flows from God to us and through us to others. Let us embark on this journey of tearing down walls and experiencing the boundless love of our Heavenly Father, Disowning the Lies.

WOULD Y○U

Marry You

Chapter 5- Let it Go

Forgiving others: *Get out of the self-made prison - Take back Control.*

Unforgiveness gives Satan the key to keep many believers imprisoned to the past because they fail to forgive others as Christ has forgiven them. Forgiveness is the tool we can use; to not only find happiness, but the key to free us from a prison of resentment and anger. It's unfortunate that the "Lord's Prayer" has become so routine that we don't realize our actual plea. "Forgive us our sins as we forgive those who sin against us", in other words, If I don't forgive others, don't forgive me. No matter how much someone has hurt you, you can forgive them.

We've all heard the saying forgive and forget but forgiveness is not forgetting. It is not feeling the stinger when we hear our offenders name or see their face. It's not wanting revenge.

Don't be on the same level as the abuser (Romans 12:17-

19).

Some people just want the satisfaction of hating the person. But hanging on only sickens the soul (Psalm 37:8). Trying to cover it up doesn't fool anyone because "the heart knows its own bitterness (Proverbs 14:10)." It's time to take control of the key to unlock the gate by forgiving every person that has left scars and bruises that continue to get "bumped" throughout our lives. We'll start by looking at some truths about forgiveness.

What is Forgiveness

I came across a quote about forgiveness the other day that I would like to share with you.

> *"Holding on to anger, resentment and hurt only gives you tense muscles, a headache and a sore jaw from clenching your teeth. Forgiveness gives you back the laughter and the lightness in your life".*
>
> *Joan Lunden*

We all have those days when we're clenching our teeth. Sometimes it's hard to forgive and find our way back to happiness. We feel the need to hang on to anger and hurt, and get some sort of revenge for the wrong done to us. Yet often that revenge never comes because the other person has long moved on with their life, didn't realize how much they hurt us, or really didn't care in the first place.

Sometimes we do get revenge. We get a chance to lash out and hurt back. When it's done, we feel hollow inside and realize too late that causing more pain does not cancel out the pain we receive. Instead, our time and energy would be much better spent learning to forgive and move on with our life. Are you ready to give Forgiveness a try and get the "laughter and the lightness in your life" back?

The good news is that it's something that's very achievable and well within your reach. All it takes is a decision on your part to forgive. That's a pretty powerful feeling, isn't it? Forgiveness is a choice you make that gives you full control over the situation. So often, we feel like the victim when someone hurts or takes advantage of us.

Hanging on to the anger and pain and refusing to forgive gives the other person a hold over us. Forgiveness is your choice to make. You hold all the cards. It's not always easy, but something you can do for yourself. I think it's important that we're on the same page about what forgiveness is. Forgiveness can mean a lot of different things to different people, and in different situations. Forgiveness is the act of forgiving someone or something. This could mean forgiving them for harsh words or unkind actions. It can also mean that we forgive a debt. That debt could be emotional (someone owes us a favor for example), or material and monetary (forgiving the $20 owed to you).

We'll be focusing on the emotional forgiveness. In many ways, it's much easier to forgive a material debt than an emotional one. In those cases when we have a hard time forgiving a material debt, chances are it's because strong emotions are involved as well. Take for example the many cases when siblings start to fight and drift apart while dividing up their parent's estate. Those fights and arguments aren't really about who gets mom's china or dad's toolbox. It's much more about dealing with loss, hanging on to the memories of loved ones, and making sure you get your "fair share" of that legacy.

Forgiveness then is the act of forgiving someone for something they have done to you or your perception of what they've done. It's about letting go and being able to move on. It's not about acting like nothing ever happened. Instead, it's about accepting the past so you can let go of it. It's about living in the present and looking forward to the future. It's about letting go of resentment, so you have room to let in joy and happiness.

What it boils down to is this. Forgiveness isn't really about the other person. It's about you. It's about taking back control of your life and your emotions. It's about forging your own destiny. Forgiveness really is a choice you have to make. How will you choose to deal with negativity? Will you allow it to take control over your life and how you feel? Will you allow it to shade everything else that happens to you going forward? Will you allow these bad memories to continue to play on an endless loop in your head?

Or are you ready to get back in charge, make the conscious choice to forgive, and thus take the power over your feelings and reactions away from the person who's done you wrong? Are you ready to empower yourself and free yourself from the prison you've built in the name of justice and getting even?

I hope you do. Living a life of forgiveness means living a

life filled with love, acceptance, and joy. It's not always easy to forgive, but it's always well worth it.

What Forgiveness Isn't

I shared my thoughts about what exactly forgiveness is and what it means. Now, I want to take a little bit of time to look at what forgiveness isn't and what it doesn't mean. There are a lot of common misconceptions when it comes to forgiveness and it's important that we clear some of them up before moving on. Let me quickly run you through them so you gain an even better understanding of what forgiveness is all about, and what it isn't.

Forgiveness Doesn't Mean You Excuse and Condone

When we forgive someone, we do it despite knowing that what they did was wrong and possibly hurtful. It does in no way mean that we excuse and condone their behavior or that we suddenly agree with them. Far from it. Instead, we decide to forgive despite what they've done.

Forgiveness simply means that we choose to get past it and bring closure for our own sake. Forgiveness is much more about the person doing the forgiving than the one being forgiven. It helps us to not only move past what happened, but also stop feeling grief, anger, and pain about it. It's a very freeing experience. Forgiveness is about acceptance of things we cannot change or have no control over.

Forgiveness Doesn't Mean Giving Up

To forgive someone doesn't mean that we're giving up. We can still work on finding justice or continue to work towards improving things and forgive at the same time. It simply means that we choose to let go enough that the anger, pain, and fear no longer paralyzes us.

Forgiveness is a very freeing feeling. It helps us move on with our lives; including any plans we have to make sure what happened to us doesn't happen to anyone else. It doesn't mean that we're giving in and suddenly going along with everything the other person does. In fact, we can forgive someone and continue to not spend time with them.

Forgiveness Doesn't Mean You're Weak

To be forgiving also isn't a sign of weakness. Again, the opposite is true. It takes a lot of strength and character to be able to forgive and move on. It doesn't turn you into a pushover. It shows your strength of character and faith.

Forgiveness Doesn't Let Them Get Away with It

Last but not least, don't feel like you let someone get away with it when you forgive them. You can be forgiving and understanding and still expect them to make up for what they've done. I can't stress enough how forgiveness really isn't about the other person, it's about you. It's what's going to help you move on, get back to your life, and find happiness while still doing what you have to do to set things right.

Practicing forgiveness can be hard. We don't want to forgive when we're hurt. We want the other person to pay for what they've done. Forgiving seems like we are giving in and giving up. Thankfully that's far from the truth. Instead, we can forgive because we chose to get past the pain and anger. While revenge and handing out more pain can't cancel out the pain we feel, forgiveness can help us heal.

When we're really honest we don't want revenge. We don't want to inflict more pain. What we really want is to heal and move on with our life. Practicing forgiveness will get us there. It doesn't mean that we love the person who hurt us, and it doesn't even mean that we get back to the relationship we had before. But it does mean that we give up those feelings of resentment and the need to get even in order to find peace. Forgiveness will help us heal and move on to a happier place.

Now, let's talk about what happens when you choose to ignore forgiveness, or you just plain can't bring yourself to forgive and move on. I get it. There are times and situations where it's hard to forgive. There are times when you just don't want to forgive and you're not ready to move on. And sometimes it's ok to feel resentful and angry for a little while before you are ready to forgive.

The important part is that you get yourself in a state of mind where you can forgive. You don't want to get stuck in a world of anger, resentment, and revenge. That's not a healthy place to be and it can lead to all sorts of problems. Most importantly it prevents you from moving on to a place where you can feel happy and content again.

Ignoring Forgiveness Keeps You Stuck

It's impossible to move on with your life when you are holding on to those feelings of resentment. The saddest part about being stuck when you ignore forgiveness is that chances are good that the other person has long moved on. They aren't wasting another thought on what happened. They aren't worried or feeling bad about it. They've probably forgotten all about it and moved on with their life. You on the other hand are stuck in a bad emotional place until you can find it in your heart to forgive. This right here is why forgiveness is really all about you and getting yourself unstuck.

Holding On to Anger Keeps Out Happiness

When you're holding on to that anger, it's hard to make room for more positive feelings. You know yourself that you can't be happy and angry at the same time. Practicing forgiveness makes room in your heart to let the joy and happiness back in. If that's not a great reason to make a serious effort to forgive, I don't know what is.

It May Even Cause Depression

Last but not least, when you're stuck in that dark place for too long, you may even end up depressed. Is holding on to a grudge worth risking depression? While there may be some other contributing factors when you do find yourself depressed, finding it in your heart to forgive can be very helpful. It allows you to move on and lift this burden from your chest. The freeing feeling you'll notice when you choose to forgive will go a long way towards helping you feel better. Before long you'll find yourself digging out of the whole depression creates and see the light at the end of the tunnel.

Please take this warning seriously. Ignoring forgiveness doesn't hurt anyone else more than it hurts you. Do yourself a favor and do what you need to do to forgive and move on to happier times.

The Connection Between Forgiveness & Depression
We briefly went over some of the negative things associated with ignoring forgiveness. Now, I want to dig a little deeper and take a look at the connection between forgiveness and depression. There are actually two sides to this story. One involves forgiving, or choosing to hold on to a grudge and the other involves feeling like you're not forgiving. In either case, when there is no forgiveness, the chances of either party ending up depressed are fairly high.

In other words, by choosing to not forgive, you're not only hurting yourself, but you're potentially putting the other party involved in a dark place as well. Several U.S. universities have done studies on forgiveness and depression and there seems to be a definite link between the two. The consensus seems to be that when we choose to hold on to grudges and feelings of resentment, we feel less connected and have less room for happiness and other positive feelings and experiences. As a result, depression can creep in. But there's good news…

Thankfully the connection between forgiveness and depression works both ways. If you're feeling depressed, think about what you've done and what has been done to you in the past. Then work on both giving and receiving forgiveness. Both have a very powerful impact on lifting depression and helping you feel better.

Forgiveness isn't something that comes naturally to human beings. It's a learned behavior and some of us have spent more time than others in our childhood and as young adults practicing this skill. If you find yourself lacking, now may be a great time to work on your forgiveness skills. Not only will you feel better, but you'll also ward off future episodes of depression.

Actively forgiving someone brings us closer to each other. Since we're social creatures, we crave and need those connections. They help us work well together and bring us joy and happiness. And the end result is that they can help us lift depression or prevent it in the first place.

What it boils down to is this. You have a choice. You can choose to hold on to grudges and feelings of resentment. You can hold on to anger and pain. Or you can choose to practice and embrace forgiveness, let go of that anger and pain, and in turn make room for much happier feelings. What will you choose? I hope it is a path towards forgiveness.

Forgiving self- Accepting God's forgiveness
There's one very important person we've not talked about yet – and that's you. It's about time we take a closer look at forgiving yourself, what it means, why it's so difficult, and why it is important.

Forgiving yourself is often harder than forgiving anyone else. We're hard on ourselves. We are our own worst critics and as a result it's often tough to forgive ourselves. It's hard to admit and let go of our mistakes especially when we see the negative impact and the hurt, we've caused others. Yet self-forgiveness is one of the most powerful parts of self-love.

When you learn to forgive yourself for your past

mistakes, you aren't just able to start moving on. You will also start to develop a deeper feeling of self-worth. With that comes a new-found self-confidence that will serve you well in the days to come. Life is much easier and a lot more fun when you are able to develop a good feeling of self-worth and self-confidence.

Of course, all of that is easier said than done. Forgiving yourself, as I mentioned earlier, is harder than it looks. It's not something that comes easy for most of us. If you're lacking in self-worth, and self-confidence, it will be even harder. The good news is that you can get there by following a simple step-by-step process.

Start by admitting your mistakes. You won't be able to forgive yourself if you don't know what you're forgiving yourself for. Make a list, or simply start with some of your biggest mistakes. Admit them to yourself so you can start to move on.

Next, think about what you would have done differently, given the chance. Knowing what you do now, what would you change? With that clear in your mind, realize that you did the best at the time. Maybe you didn't make the best decisions, but you had to grow as a person to realize that. Forgive your past self for the decisions you made and be thankful for those mistakes. They are part of what molded you into the person you are today. We learn from our mistakes and all experiences (good and bad), mold and shape us.

Last but not least, vow to do better in the future. You have grown and become a different (and hopefully better) person as a result of the mistakes you've made. Forgive yourself for the things you regret and work on doing better going forward. Do this and you'll notice how your feeling of self-worth increases with each good decision you make. Before you know it, you'll be the confident, happy person you're striving to be – thanks to self-forgiveness.

Write down any names or faces that come to your mind. Most begin this list with "mother, father, spouse, teachers, etc. Don't question whether you need to forgive them, trust the Holy Spirit.

For every painful memory that God reveals for each person on your list, pray aloud:

Prayer of Forgiveness towards Others (pray this prayer aloud for each person God revealed)

Lord Jesus, I choose to forgive {name the person} for {what he or she did or failed to do} because it made me feel {share the painful feelings; rejected, unloved, dirty, worthless, etc.}. Lord, I choose not to hold on to my resentment. I relinquish my right to seek revenge and ask You to heal my damaged emotions. Thank You for setting me free from the bondage of my bitterness. Thank You for the key that unlocked the chains that kept me bound to my offender by my choice to not forgive. I now ask You to bless those who have hurt me. In Jesus' name, I pray. Amen

This concept of "letting go" of anger, guilt, and condemnation toward self is something rooted in our failure to understand God's cleansing and forgiveness.

Only God can forgive our sins, which separate us from Him, and He has. But we need to forgive ourselves for our failures, for letting God down, and for hurting others. Otherwise, we believe the subtle deception that we must atone for our own sins.

Dear Heavenly Father, I thank You for loving me more than I could ever truly understand. You are a good-good Father and I want to represent You in all that I do. I want to be an example of your grace, mercy, and love. I confess that I have beat myself up for things that I have done or failed to do even after asking for Your forgiveness. Your word says that if I confess my sins, You are just to forgive me. Instead, I have held onto anger, bitterness, and resentment toward myself and because of the guilt and shame I have allowed the condemnation of the enemy to dictate how I treat myself and others. Please bring to mind the things I need to deal with. In Jesus' name I pray. Amen

Believers that continue to "beat themselves up" are being victimized by Satan, or by their own misperceptions of self, rather than the truth of God's grace. Forgiving ourselves is giving ourselves permission to receive forgiveness from God. Forgiving ourselves is saying in effect, "Lord, I believe that You have forgiven me and cleansed me of my sins through Your Son. Because of Your great love and grace - not because I deserve it - I choose to no longer condemn myself when You have forgiven me. I receive your forgiveness and cleansing."

Prayer of Forgiveness towards Self (pray this prayer aloud for each area God revealed)

Lord Jesus, I choose not to hold on to my resentment and bitterness against myself for _____ . I refuse to blame, condemn and house bitterness against myself because of my past mistakes, and I ask You to heal my damaged emotions. I receive the forgiveness and grace of God that covers and cleanses me from my sins. Thank You for setting me free from the bondage of guilt, shame from my past experiences. In Jesus' name I pray. Amen

Bitterness toward God is far more common than most people would care to admit. But when they become honest about their anger toward God, another stronghold begins to crumble. Satan's scheme is to turn us against God by raising up thoughts against Him (2 Corinthians 10:4-5). They cause us to rebel against His Lordship. Satan is defeated when we release God from our own false expectations and stop blaming Him for our own failures or things that we perceive is not working in our favor.

Dear Heavenly Father, I thank You for continuing to love me and extend grace and patience. I confess there have been times when I was not happy with the way things happened in my life and others and I turned that anger, disappointment, and frustration toward You. It is not something I am proud of, but I know if I don't get honest, open, and transparent about how I have felt, I can't heal. I have allowed the enemy access to my thoughts through this, and I choose today to take back control. Please bring to mind every time I have not been in Your will in this area. In Jesus' name I pray. Amen

Write down any areas where you are bitter towards God. People don't always forgive because of actual offense;

they forgive for what they "think" has been done to them. Bitterness isn't always rooted in reality; it is sometimes rooted in perceptions. That is why it is not wrong to "forgive" thoughts toward God. Of course, God has never done anything wrong and there is no need to "forgive", but you must release any bitterness you have held against God for things that didn't turn out the way you expected. When people have worked through their bitterness toward God, they immediately acknowledge the fact that God hasn't done anything wrong. Working through the bitterness toward God brings tremendous healing and restoration.

Prayer of Forgiveness towards God (pray this prayer for each specific area mentioned above)

Lord Jesus, I choose not to hold on to my resentment and bitterness against God for _____.
I relinquish the right to blame God and I ask You to heal my damaged emotions. Father, I know You know what is best in every situation. Help me to accept Your will in all things. Help my unbelief, doubt, and fear. Please forgive me for not trusting You. Thank You for setting me free. In Jesus' name I pray. Amen

Chapter 6: Purpose Gives Permission

"Who have you allowed to name you?" and "What name are you answering to?"

Romans 8:28 reminds us that God causes all things to work together for the good of those who love Him and are called according to His purpose for them. This powerful verse serves as a guiding light, emphasizing the importance of understanding our purpose, as it allows us to find value and meaning in our lives. Just like an item at a yard sale with no label or instructions, our purpose, value, and name can only be determined by our Creator.

Imagine wandering through a yard sale, picking up an item with a torn package, no price tag, or instructions, and thinking, "What is this used for?" Or "How much is this worth?" Maybe you wonder, "What on earth do you call this thing?" The purpose, value, and name are unknown because it is separated from the source of the answers to these questions. There is nothing available to determine its identity.

This situation often reflects how we feel in life when we are unsure of our purpose. We may ask others or seek validation from the world, but true purpose can only come from our Creator. Just like the ratchet tool example, its true value wasn't revealed until its purpose was exposed based on its identity. Similarly, there are countless stories of antiques being sold for pennies, only to realize later that they are worth millions. The value couldn't be determined because there wasn't a name on the painting, and it was separated from the artist, the creator. However, once the painting was identified with the artist and named, its true value was placed on it.

In the beginning, Adam was given the task of naming all things created by God. In direct relationship and constant communication with the Creator, he named everything from a pure, undefiled place. God decided that he needed a helper to carry out the assignment, and once created, she was brought to him to name. The man named her woman because she was created from his rib, making her a part of him. He named her based on her identity, as she was bone of his bone. She was created by God from a part of Adam with the purpose of helping him expand, rule, and manage the garden. Their purpose was clear until they were separated from the Creator through sin. In that separation, they lost sight of their true identity and purpose.

Now, separated from Truth, we have to reconnect with the Creator to seek His original intent for our lives. Spend time looking at your journey and see the things that have been given permission to impact your life, both good and bad, then ask how they work together for your good. Shift your thinking from things happening to you to things happening for you. What picture do you see when you put the puzzle pieces of your journey together?

Began to seek the face of the Lord to discover your purpose (His original intent). It won't be long before He reveals why He created you and every pain you've experienced had a purpose. They were strategically designed to prepare you for His purpose. This discovery will lead you to the relationships, career paths, and areas that are designed to help you become the best version of yourself so you can be fruitful and multiply.

Understanding your purpose becomes even more critical when considering relationships, especially the covenant of marriage. Let's take a moment to look at the life of the Noble Wife of Proverbs 31, an exemplary figure of a woman who knew her purpose and walked confidently in it.

She knew who she was and had a deep relationship with God. This relationship served as the foundation for her identity and purpose. As a result, she was respected and praised yet remained humble in her actions.

She could be trusted, knowing the importance of being faithful and dependable. Her stewardship extended to her home, where she managed it well by giving instructions to her servant girls. She understood the value of teamwork and accepting help.

The Noble Wife was an entrepreneur, engaging in various business ventures, inspecting, selling, and buying. She demonstrated wisdom and discernment in her decision-making, ensuring her business deals were profitable.

Not only did she take care of herself physically, but she also extended her arms to the needy, always ready to help those in distress. Her compassion and generosity flowed from her understanding of her purpose and her trust in God.

Most importantly, the Noble Wife feared the Lord. Her relationship with God was the core of her identity, and she knew she was in a covenant relationship with Him. This deep reverence for God guided her actions, decisions, and interactions with others.

In studying the life of the Noble Wife, we discover that she embodied her purpose. She was confident in her calling, diligent in her work, and compassionate in her service. Her identity was firmly rooted in God, giving her the strength and wisdom to fulfill her purpose.

In the story of Ruth, we find a beautiful illustration of a woman walking in her purpose. Ruth, a Moabite woman, was widowed and chose to remain loyal to her mother-in-law, Naomi, and accompany her back to Israel. There, she found herself gleaning in the fields, picking up the leftover grain after the harvesters. This simple act of gleaning may not have seemed significant, but it was a vital part of Ruth's purpose.

As she gleaned in the fields, Ruth caught the attention of Boaz, the owner of the fields and a close relative of

Naomi's late husband. Boaz noticed Ruth's faithfulness, humility, and hard work. He saw her aligning with her purpose, diligently providing for her family. Boaz recognized her worth and even referred to her as "a woman of noble character" (Ruth 3:11).

Boaz, being a man of integrity, went on to fulfill his role as the kinsman-redeemer. He redeemed Ruth and Naomi from their difficult circumstances, marrying Ruth and securing their future. Ruth's purpose of loyalty, hard work, and faithfulness led her to her divine destiny.

In our own lives, it is essential to recognize that our actions, no matter how insignificant they may seem, are all part of our purpose. Whether it's in the workplace, in our relationships, or in our daily interactions with others, our purpose is woven into every aspect of our lives.

As we align with our purpose and walk confidently in God's plan, we find ourselves attracting the right people and opportunities. Just like Ruth caught Boaz's attention by being faithful to her purpose, when we are true to our calling, we attract those who recognize our value and respect our journey.

Now, I ask you again: Are you ready to "Get Ready" and embrace your purpose? Discover the beauty of who God created you to be, and when asked the question, "Would You Marry You?" be able to confidently say YES. Just like Ruth and the Nobel Wife, may you walk faithfully in your purpose, attracting the right people and fulfilling your divine destiny.

As you read "The Purpose Driven Life" by Rick Warren, you'll discover the five purposes God has designed for your life:

1. Worship: Created to bring glory to God and have a personal relationship with Him through worship and praise.
2. Ministry: Created to serve others and use your unique gifts and talents to make a difference in the lives of those around you.
3. Evangelism: Created to share the Good News of Jesus Christ with others and bring them into a personal relationship with Him.
4. Discipleship: Created to grow spiritually and become more like Christ through study, prayer, and fellowship with other believers.
5. Fellowship: Created to be part of a community of believers, supporting and encouraging one another on the journey of faith.

As you align your life with these five purposes, you'll find fulfillment, joy, and a deeper connection to God. Embracing your purpose gives you the confidence to walk in God's plan, making you a person who knows their identity and worth.

So, I encourage you to embark on this journey of purpose, seeking the face of the Lord, and discovering the divine plan He has for your life. May you find the courage to embrace your purpose, allowing it to guide your decisions, actions, and interactions with others. Let the story of Ruth and the Nobel Wife remind you that when you walk confidently in your purpose, you attract the right people and opportunities, ultimately fulfilling your God-given destiny. Trust in His design for your life, and you will find joy, fulfillment, and a deeper sense of purpose that brings glory to His name.

Based on the wisdom and guidance from the book "The Purpose Driven Life" by Rick Warren, the S.H.A.P.E process is a powerful tool to help you identify and embrace your unique purpose. Understanding your S.H.A.P.E will enable you to align your life with God's design, finding fulfillment and meaning in every aspect of your existence.

S - Spiritual Gifts: Begin by exploring the spiritual gifts that God has given you. These are special abilities and talents that the Holy Spirit imparts to believers for the purpose of serving others and building up the body of Christ. Reflect on the areas where you excel, the tasks that come naturally to you, and the ways you have experienced God's power at work in your life. Embrace your spiritual gifts and consider how you can use them to serve others and bring glory to God.

H - Heart: Your heart represents your passions and desires. What issues, causes, or activities ignite a fire within you? Consider the things that make your heart come alive and the areas where you feel a deep sense of compassion and concern. Your heart's desires are often connected to your purpose, as God plants these passions in you to guide you towards the path, He has designed for you.

A - Abilities: Explore your natural talents and abilities. These are the skills and aptitudes that you have honed over time and can be used to make a positive impact on others. Your abilities complement your spiritual gifts and provide practical means to fulfill your purpose. Consider the skills you have developed through education, experience, and practice, and seek ways to utilize them for the benefit of others.

P - Personality: Your personality traits and temperament play a significant role in how you relate to others and approach various aspects of life. Consider whether you are an introvert or an extrovert, how you handle challenges, and how you communicate with others. Understanding your personality will help you find the most effective and fulfilling ways to express your purpose and serve others.

E - Experiences: Your life experiences, both positive and negative, shape and prepare you for your purpose. Reflect on the challenges you have overcome, the lessons you have learned, and the transformative moments in your journey. God can use these experiences to equip you for specific tasks and to empathize with others who face similar struggles. Embrace your life experiences and allow them to fuel your purpose-driven journey.

By exploring your S.H.A.P.E - your Spiritual Gifts, Heart, Abilities, Personality, and Experiences - you will gain a clearer understanding of how God has uniquely designed you for a specific purpose. Embrace your S.H.A.P.E as a gift from God and commit to using it to serve others, impact lives, and bring glory to His name.

As you walk in alignment with your S.H.A.P.E, you will discover a deep sense of fulfillment and joy, knowing that you are living out your God-given purpose. Allow God to guide and direct your steps, and trust that He will use your S.H.A.P.E to bring about His divine plan for your life. Embrace your purpose and impact the world and every relationship with the unique contribution only you can make.

WOULD YOU
Marry You

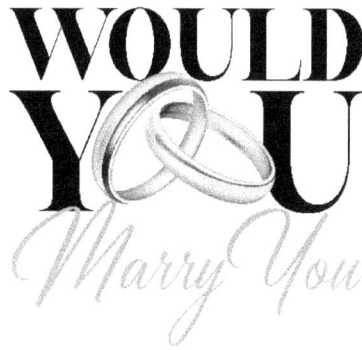

Chapter 7: CONCLUSION

In conclusion, I would like to share an excerpt from a book written by my very 1st client (with permission). I pray her story encourages you that you are good soil to invest the time to heal and "Get Ready".

One dreary day some years ago, the call came, "You have to leave town as soon as possible. Lee told me to get my black dress ready because when he finds you, he's going to put a bullet in your head!" Wow, he's going to take it this far. 7-months pregnant with his child and he's really going to kill me. Why should I be surprised? I should have expected this after having him hold a gun to my head months prior. I knew the day would come when I would have to leave, I just thought I had more time. The shelter had been so helpful, and I was in my own place. See, months prior, I began implementing my exit strategy. The first step was reaching out to my estranged husband, to come get the oldest two children. The next step was going to a battered women's shelter where I could be safe, get counseling, and help to acquire a place of my own so my babies could come back home. This is where I met my 1st Counselor/Coach. She called me out on my BS and made me look at me. She gave me these handouts with all these questions, didn't she know I don't have time for all this. I had just found out that I was expecting my 4th child. I was angry, hurt, confused, and scared. Thoughts were racing through my head; "Now you can never get away from him," "He's going to find you," "You will never be safe."

All the thoughts appear to be coming true as he's now calling with threats. Once the shock of this disturbing message began to subside, my analytical thinking kicked into high gear. 'I must go home, pack our things and leave the state. But where will I go?' As I was processing and speaking my thoughts aloud, Marie made it clear that she didn't think it was a good idea to go to my house, but I refused to listen. I took the baby to her place and headed to my own. As I put my key into the lock to open the door, the entire door fell inward. He had removed the hinges and propped the door back as if it were okay. He'd found me! I alerted my neighbor who graciously agreed to go in with me. We found that all our clothes were gone. He had taken everything. The house had been ransacked, the baby's medicine and breathing machine were gone. The dresser drawers were all over the room, closets emptied, food dumped over the kitchen and

WOULD YOU MARRY YOU

cabinets emptied. Broken glass and trash littered the entire place. He'd found me!

Fear began to rise up inside me. After expressing the situation to my estranged husband, I informed him that I was coming to get the kids and we would be going West where the family could help me. He said, "I'm sorry I placed you in this situation, come back to me and we will work things out, you are still my wife." So, 7-months pregnant, an asthmatic baby that had just turned 1yr old, in a five speed Ford Escort with literally the clothes on our backs, we set out down the highway to the promise of "let's start over" once again.

See, just a short 18 months prior, our family of 4 migrated North after a series of adulterous affairs on his part. This was supposed to be a "let's start over" season of our lives. There had been so much physical, emotional, spiritual, and psychological abuse in the South, I agreed to "give it one more try" up North. A fresh start where neither of us had a past. I was determined to make this work. Things looked as if they were going well, however, less than 3 months into this new venture, he comes in from work and says, "I don't want to be married anymore but we have to stay together for the kid's sake. I have found someone else, and you need to do the same."

WHAT, I thought this was our "fresh start"!!!! A new place, no history for either of us and now this! On comes depression, the deepest, darkest, scariest time of my life, thus far. I couldn't eat, couldn't sleep, couldn't stop crying. Those seeds of rejection, abandonment, betrayal, unloved, used, hopelessness and helplessness were being watered and I didn't know how much longer I could take this. I was answering each one as if they were my name. I owned them. They were my identity, and I was operating based on what I believed to be true about me. Who was wrong with me? Me and the narcissists that I had allowed to name me. I was hours from checking myself into a mental hospital when the neighbor noticed something wrong. She reached out and invited me to a jazz event where I met someone that called me by a different name. One that felt good. However, that name opened my eyes to a world that I had only read about in books and seen in gangster movies. He was a bad boy, and I was liking it.

Through a series of events, I found myself 4 months pregnant, not sure if my son belonged to my husband or my bad boy lover who was in jail for an undetermined length of time by this time. I got my own place for the 1st time in my life along with my children. Things were going well. The healing process had begun toward my husband, and it appeared that maybe there was a chance of reconciliation. Then it happened, yet another woman pops up. "DONE" That's it. So much for this whole commitment thing. With bitterness in my heart from the continual disregard for my emotions, I decided to take control. I will just fulfill fleshly needs without commitment and there's a guy outside that can help me out with that. Hints the beginning of the year of Lee, as I call it. Yeah, about that, this whole non-commitment thing kind of didn't work out so well for me, my life is being threatened and I'm running from the consequences of my own sin.

Now here I am heading back to the husband like a puppy with its tail tucked between its legs. His words from years prior vibrated in my head, "Nobody's going to want you with kids," "You're only safe with me," "You are my wife until we die," "You must submit to me" "you can't do anything right." Well, here I go again with the promise looming "We will be a family again" as my motivation. I arrived and headed straight to the ER as my baby boy is now struggling to breathe since he had not had medicine for over 24 hrs. Determined to surprise the hubby, I didn't call anyone. After the ER visit, we proceeded to surprise him only to walk into the house and find him in bed with yet another woman…. My heart sank! I hurried out of the house before he saw me or my reaction. How could this be?

As I pulled off, I flipped the mirror down to look at myself. There appeared to be words plastered on my forehead: failure, stupid, betrayed, unworthy of being loved, rejected, abandoned, used, hopeless and helpless. The names I again answered to. The sign appeared to say "Narcist Magnet" What is wrong with me?

I began to read the prayer my counselor/coach from the shelter gave me, Lord, even now, I know I am Your child. I am Your baby girl. You are a good Father. You love me above anything I can ever imagine, and I worship You alone. You are amazing. You sit high and look low and love me too much to leave me where I am and for that Father, I say Thank You. Thank you for the blood of your Son, Jesus, who was shed for the forgiveness of my sins, to set me free, and to reverse the works of the devil. I confess that I have done things that You have commanded me not to do and I have not done all that You have commanded me to do and for this Father, I am truly sorry. I repent of my wicked ways by turning my heart, mind and will toward you. I thank You Lord for your forgiveness and I choose to forgive myself. (then added my own part) Now give me the grace to forgive ML and Lee that I may be set free and begin to heal. I don't feel loved right now. Please show me who you say I am. In Jesus name, I pray, Amen.

The stress of all that had taken place in the previous days landed me in labor 6 weeks early. I gave birth to a beautiful baby girl. The placenta had released from my uterus and protruded through my cervix. A few hours more and she would have been stillborn due to a lack of oxygen and nutrients. I was all alone in a state where I'd been betrayed. How did I get here?

Yet, I'm getting ready to board a Greyhound bus alone with my babies to begin a new life some 15.5hrs away.

The bus ride with 4 babies was interesting, but God let them sleep most of the time and sent angels to help me with bathroom breaks and diaper changes. While they slept, I cried and prayed.

Over everybody of water, I did what my counselor/coach taught me; "toss all your cares, concerns, and worries into the water and allow it to take them far away." I prayed, "Father please break any ties I have to anyone from my past. Let me not desire to contact or communicate with anyone from my past. I want to be free of those connections and be open to all you have for me." He told me to throw out my phonebook, yes, I still had one of those, so I did. It was probably one of the hardest things to do, but I knew I couldn't move forward while looking through the rearview mirror. On the other side of forgiveness, obedience, and repentance he was naming me, he had given permission to everything that had taken place and I was ready to start walking in the truth of His original intent for my life!

I arrived with a new sense of humility that took over as I was going back into my mothers' home as a married woman with 4 children. I returned as a child with childlike faith, totally submitted to whatever God had in store for me. Having time to forgive all who had hurt me, the healing of my soul was taking place and I was able to start really seeing myself through God's eyes.

In three short months I managed to get a job, my own

place, and establish a church home. Shortly after I publicly rededicated my life and was rebaptized truly understanding what it meant to accept Jesus as Lord, not just Savior.

I was not what I had done. I was not what others had called me. I was not what I had been through. I was who he said I was. I had returned to God and was identified with my creator who had determined my value, purpose and named me. He called me Daughter, not servant. He showed me who I was to Him, so I had to disown the lies I had believed about myself.

Four years later, while my heart was still being healed by renewing my mind, stewarding the power of my tongue, and applying Kingdom Revelation through obedience I started my online business. I remember Coach telling me to follow the guide of Proverbs 31 wife. Because I listened to God and did my research it didn't take long for me to have my 1st $5000 month. I had no idea how to manage that kind of money, so I hired another coach. One of the most important things my 1st coach taught me was that I could shortcut the learning curve by investing in Coaching and Mentoring. She convinced me that I was good soil to invest time and money in to progress and move from Orphan Spirit to Beloved Child and from Poverty Spirit to Inheritance of Kingdom promise.

My new coach (Entrepreneur) was amazing and very knowledgeable about business structure and accounting processes, and he wasn't half bad looking either. I found out I needed to restructure a lot of things as well as hire a Virtual Assistant so I could work on the business and not in it. He was so super helpful and the 12 weeks we worked together passed very quickly.

On our very last appointment he asked if I would like to join him for a jazz event, which of course I said yes. Well one date led to another and six months later, he asked me to spend the rest of my life as his wife, which of course I said yes. We just celebrated our 12th Anniversary and are car shopping for our youngest child who will be 16 soon. I'm so happy I took the time and invested in me so I could "Get Ready" to be that good thing he found.

I thank God, I had the tools I needed for the journey. A special thank you to my Counselor/Coach from the shelter. I pray she never stops calling people out on their BS. (Belief Systems) ~ Anonymous.

BONUS TRUTH ENCOUNTER- DELIVERANCE

1. Redemption History

In the beginning, God formed humanity in His image, breathing life into them both physically and spiritually. Adam and Eve were beautifully crafted in the likeness of God (Genesis 1:27). Placed in the exquisite Garden of Eden, they were entrusted with the responsibility to rule over all creation and were blessed to be fruitful and multiply (Genesis 1:28). Their souls were intimately connected to their bodies, and their spirits were deeply united with God. This divine union made Adam and Eve feel secure, cherished, and significant. God granted them access to every tree in the garden, except the Tree of the Knowledge of Good and Evil, as a test of their obedience and trust (Genesis 2:15-17).

Before humanity's creation, a celestial being named Lucifer, consumed by jealousy, rebelled against the Almighty God and was cast out of heaven, taking a third of the angels with him (Isaiah 14:12-15). This fallen angel became known as Satan, the devil, who ruled over the fallen angels, now called demons. Satan, desiring the elevated position Adam and Eve held, cunningly tempted Eve to partake of the forbidden fruit in the Garden of Eden. Eve, in turn, persuaded Adam to do the same, and together they defied God's command, sinning against Him (Genesis 3:1-6).

As a consequence of their disobedicncc, Adam and Eve experienced an immediate spiritual death, a separation from God. They found themselves lost, searching for their purpose and identity apart from their Heavenly Father. Stripped of the life of God within them, they had to rely solely on their own strength and resources (Genesis 3:17-19). From that moment forward, every descendant of Adam and Eve entered the world physically alive but spiritually dead.

God's intricate plan involved revealing to humanity their dire need for a Savior who could reverse the consequences of the Fall. He demonstrated this need through the institution of a sacrificial system, known as the Law of Moses found in the book of Leviticus. This system illustrated that someone had to pay the price for our sins in order to restore our union with God (Hebrews 9:22). However, animal sacrifices were incapable of bestowing spiritual life upon us, and no one could perfectly fulfill the requirements of the Law.

Just when it seemed all hope was lost, God sent forth His Son, Jesus (Romans 8:3). Jesus, supernaturally conceived by the Virgin Mary (Isaiah 7:14), came into the world fully alive both physically and spiritually, just like Adam.

Jesus was the Word of God incarnate, dwelling among us (John 1:14). He embarked on His earthly mission for three primary purposes:

1. Jesus came to exemplify how a spiritually alive individual could lead a righteous life. He demonstrated absolute dependence on His Heavenly Father, serving as our ultimate example (John 5:30). Temptation constantly tempts us to live independently of God, yet Jesus, unlike Adam, triumphed over every temptation without sinning (Hebrews 4:15).

2. Jesus came to restore our union with God. As the sinless Lamb of God, He willingly sacrificed Himself on the cross, bearing the penalty for our sins, so that we could experience forgiveness and reconciliation (Ephesians 1:3-7). Through His resurrection, Jesus provided us with new, eternal spiritual life. Adam and Eve lost their spiritual life, their union with God, through the Fall, but Jesus came to restore that spiritual life, that union with God. He is the ONLY way back to the Father (John 14:6).

3. Jesus came to undo the works of Satan. Through His death and resurrection, Jesus disarmed Satan, conquering sin and death (Revelation 1:18). Now, all authority in heaven and on earth has been bestowed upon Jesus (Matthew 28:18). Through our union with God in Christ, we possess the authority and power to fulfill God's will on earth, making disciples and teaching them to embrace all His teachings (Matthew 28:19-20).

We can enter into this new life only by placing our complete faith and trust in God, relying solely on the redemptive work of Christ to save us (Romans 10:9-13). If you have not yet received this remarkable gift from God, why not do so right now? If you confess with your mouth, "**Jesus is Lord**," and believe in your heart that God raised him from the dead, you will be saved. For it is with your heart that you believe and are justified, and it is with your mouth that you confess and are saved. Pray this and ask God to come into your heart and Holy Spirit to guide you into all truth.

If you have sincerely prayed and accepted by faith the free gift of salvation through Jesus Christ, welcome to the everlasting life. This new life in Christ (2 Corinthians 5:17), our union with God, is often referred to in the Bible as being "in Christ" or "in Him." By the grace of God, not by our own works, we are now deemed "saints," set apart and sacred, and we become part of the greater "Body of Christ."

To repent means to change both our mindset and our behavior will soon follow. We are saved by God's grace through faith in the finished work of Christ (Ephesians 2:4-5). However, if we truly desire to experience the fullness of our new life and freedom in Christ and grow by God's grace, we must repent of our sins (2 Corinthians 7:10). Our newfound belief in our identity "in Christ" should manifest in our daily lives. After Jesus ascended to glory, He sent the Holy Spirit to all who believed in His finished work (John 14:16). The Holy Spirit, the Spirit of Truth, dwells within every believer, guiding us in the Christian journey from the moment we experience spiritual rebirth. He leads us into all truth (John 16:13), liberating us from falsehood (John 8:32). The remainder of this study will take us through the transformative process of repentance, uncovering truth in our minds, bodies, and souls.

2.   The Need to Renounce

When you follow anything that contradicts the Word of God, you are embracing false guidance. Whether it's superstition or astrology, if it relies on anything other than God, it is falsehood. The Word of God instructs us to place our trust solely in Him. Therefore, we must renounce our dependence on anything contrary to His truth. Renouncing is the first step towards repentance. Repentance means changing our minds, but it is a comprehensive transformation. Repentance cannot be complete without renunciation. To turn away from old ways, we must abandon the spiritual belief systems we have operated under, change our minds to believe in the truth of God's Word, and then walk in that truth (Micah 4:5).

At the time of salvation, many faiths make a public declaration: "I renounce you, Satan, and all your works and ways." However, this is often a general statement. To truly be free from the past, we must specifically renounce every false religion, false teacher, false practice, and every form of false guidance we have participated in. We cannot believe in the truth of God while clinging to a lie. Many Christians struggle because they merely add a little Jesus to their old belief systems. They fail to grasp that the cross dealt with the forgiveness of our sins, the resurrection brought new life in Christ, and the ascension of Christ to the right hand of the Father gave us the authority and power to live victoriously in Christ. That's why we should renounce the lies and boldly declare the truth of God.

The Apostle Paul warned that in the latter times, some would turn away from the faith, embracing deceiving spirits and doctrines of demons (1 Timothy 4:1). Jesus also warned that false Christs and false prophets would arise, performing great signs and wonders to mislead even the elect, if possible (Matthew 24:24). These are counterfeit truths, appearing to be true but inspired by Satan. When discerning between truth and counterfeit, keep these things in mind:

1. Any person or group that cannot or will not declare that Jesus Christ is the Son of God should be viewed with suspicion (1 John 4:1-3). Many can acknowledge that Jesus is Lord, but they refuse to make Him their Lord (even the devil knows Jesus is Lord).
2. Any person or group that offers salvation or enlightenment through means other than the finished work of Christ is peddling counterfeit truths (Acts 4:12; 1 John 5:11-12).
3. Any person or group that promises a superior quality of life, knowledge, or special powers through any means other than a relationship with God through Jesus and submission to the Holy Spirit is involved in the occult (Acts 17:29-31). The occult operates in hidden darkness, while God does everything in the light.

Genuine repentance is how we experience true freedom. We renounce the lies of false, satanic, or worldly doctrines and embrace the truth of the gospel of Jesus Christ.

As believers, it is our responsibility to submit to God and resist the devil (James 4:7). This acknowledges God's authority over our lives and His authority over the demonic realm. In the book of Acts, there is a story about the Sons of Sceva (Acts 19:13-16). These men attempted to cast out demons in the name of Jesus, but they were not in a genuine relationship with Him and were using false teachings. The authority and power we have over the demonic realm stem from our direct connection to the Father through the blood of His Son, Jesus. Just like the new Christians in Ephesus (Acts 19:18-19), openly confessing our involvement in ungodly guidance and following it with repentant actions is the verbal stand needed to overcome false guidance. The enemy cannot read our minds, but he can hear our words.

God knows what needs to be brought into the light. There are things we may have participated in or observed that unknowingly gave a foothold to the enemy in our lives. That's why, in our prayers, we ask God to bring to mind the things we need to renounce. This first step accomplishes two important objectives:

1. It exposes and breaks mental strongholds that originated from false belief systems as we verbally renounce them in agreement with God.
2. It equips us to handle lies and strongholds that may surface later, enabling us to recognize counterfeits.

The initial step towards experiencing freedom in Christ is to renounce (verbally reject) any involvement, past or present, with occult practices, false religions, or cult teachings. This includes renouncing any oaths, vows, secret initiations, ceremonies, pacts, or covenants. God does not take false guidance lightly. "As for the person who turns to mediums and spiritists...I will set my face against him and cut him off from his people" (Leviticus 20:6).

As you find a quiet place to pray these prayers, the Lord will bring events to your mind that you may have forgotten. If He brings them up, renounce them. He knows what is granting permission to the enemy and preventing you from experiencing true freedom in Him.

Dear Heavenly Father, please bring to my mind anything and everything that I have done knowingly or unknowingly that involves occult, cult, or false religious teachings or practices. I want to experience Your freedom by renouncing any and all false guidance. In Jesus' name I pray. Amen

As He brings these things to mind write them down on a piece of paper then pray:

Lord Jesus, I confess that I have participated in (specifically name every belief and involvement with all that you have checked on the spiritual checklist), and I renounce them all as counterfeits. Thank You that in Christ I am forgiven. I pray that You will fill me with Your Holy Spirit that I may be guided by You. Amen.

3. **Believing the Truth and Overcoming Deception**

Believing the truth about who Christ is, why He came, and who we are in Him forms the foundation of our freedom. As Jesus prepared to depart from Earth, He prayed to the Father, saying, "I do not ask You to take them out of the world, but to keep them from the evil one" (John 17:15). He further prayed, "Sanctify them in the truth; Your word is truth" (v.17). This prayer reveals the pathway to freedom. The Word of God declares, "If you abide in My word, you are truly My disciples; and you will know the truth, and the truth will set you free" (John 8:31-32). Knowing the truth becomes our primary defense against the father of lies. The truth of God must penetrate our hearts to bring lasting change and freedom.

We are called to speak the truth in love and walk in the light, which means our lives should be transparent before God and others. Anything less is living a lie. Many desire to conceal their weaknesses, but hidden wounds cannot be healed. The first step towards healing, recovery, and deliverance is to step out of denial and face the truth. Truth is never an enemy; it is always a liberating friend. As Christians, we must embrace the truth. "If we say that we have fellowship with Him and yet walk in the darkness, we lie and do not practice the truth; but if we walk in the light, as He Himself is in the light, we have fellowship with one another, and the blood of Jesus His Son cleanses us from all sin" (1 John 1:6-7). In Christ, there is no darkness. Jesus is the truth, and He sets honest people free.

Jesus describes Satan as the father of lies: "Whenever he speaks a lie, he speaks from his own nature, for he is a liar and the father of lies" (John 8:44). There is no truth in him. He distorts the truth, even using Scripture, as he attempted to tempt Jesus in the desert, urging Him to act independently of His Father. He employs the same tactics with us. While he cannot change our position in Christ, he will lie and deceive. If he can make us doubt who we are in Christ, we will remain in bondage to sins that have already been forgiven. When these lies are exposed, Satan's power over the believer is broken.

The battle occurs in the mind, and Satan will do whatever it takes to make us question the truth. True freedom does not come from merely swatting at demons; it comes from dealing with sin. In this step, we employ the truth to "destroy arguments and every lofty opinion raised against the knowledge of God, and take every thought captive to obey Christ" (2 Corinthians 10:4-5). We overcome the father of lies by choosing the truth. Our task is not to dispel darkness but to turn on the light.

As believers, it is our responsibility to face reality and place our faith in God. True biblical faith is choosing to believe and act upon what is true because God declares it to be so, and He is the Truth. The more we understand the depth of God's love, power, and protection, the more we trust Him. As we recognize His complete acceptance of us in Christ, we become free to be honest, open, and, in a healthy way, vulnerable before God and others. Faith is not merely a feeling but a decision. Believing something does not make it true; rather, it is true, and we choose to believe it. Everyone lives by faith. The distinction lies in the object of our faith. God has proven Himself trustworthy, and as we renew our minds with His Word, the evidence becomes increasingly clear. Before we came to Christ, we developed defense mechanisms to protect ourselves—or so we thought. We were deceived by ourselves, the devil, and the world. We wrongly defended ourselves because Christ was not our source of defense. Unfortunately, there is no "clear" button to erase the habits we formed while living independent of our Heavenly Father. Now our faith rests in the finished work of Christ, and we must continually renew our minds with His truth.

Dear Heavenly Father, You are the truth, and I desire to live by faith according to Your truth. The truth will set me free, but in many ways I have been deceived by the father of lies, the philosophies of this fallen world, and I have deceived myself. I choose to walk in the light, knowing that You love and accept me just as I am. As I consider areas of possible deception, I invite the Spirit of truth to guide me into all truth. Please protect me from all deception as You "search me, O God, and know my heart; try me and know my anxious thoughts; and lead me in the everlasting way" (Psalm 139:23-24). In the name of Jesus I pray. Amen

As He reveals, confess the areas of deception, and ask God to show you His truth in His word.

4. **Overcoming Unforgiveness and Releasing Bitterness**

Unforgiveness among Christians grants Satan his greatest access to the Church, and many believers remain bound to their past because they have failed to forgive others as Christ has forgiven them. It is unfortunate that the "Lord's Prayer" has become so routine that we overlook its true essence. When we pray, "Forgive us our sins as we forgive those who sin against us," we are essentially asking God not to forgive us if we refuse to forgive others.

Some people react negatively to the idea of forgiving others because it seems to challenge their sense of justice. They view forgiveness as a sign of weakness, believing that it gives the offender a "green light" to continue hurting them. On the contrary, forgiveness is an act of courage that reflects the grace of God. Forgiveness does not mean tolerating sin. God forgives, but He does not tolerate sin. Forgiving others is something we do for our own sake, and resistance dissipates when we understand its true nature and how to practice it.

Some individuals resist forgiveness because they seek revenge. Seeking revenge allows the devil to set the agenda (Ephesians 4:27) and places us on the same level as the one who hurt us. It illegitimately assumes God's role of dispensing justice (Romans 12:17-19). Some people simply desire the satisfaction of hating the wrongdoer. However, clinging to bitterness only poisons the soul (Psalm 37:8). Attempting to cover it up fools no one, especially ourselves, for "the heart knows its own bitterness" (Proverbs 14:10).

While it is undeniable that you have been deeply

wounded, the path to healing involves releasing your grip on the person and allowing God to deal with them justly and fairly. When you choose forgiveness, you set both yourself and the offender free. Are you ready to make the choice and experience true freedom?

While we may be able to recall or identify someone we need to forgive, God knows them all. Let us take a moment to pray and ask God to reveal to our minds those individuals whom we need to forgive. Let us not solely rely on our memory, as we may unconsciously gloss over events or individuals to avoid the emotional pain associated with them. Therefore, let us join in prayer, seeking the guidance of the Holy Spirit.

Dear Heavenly Father, I am grateful for the richness of Your kindness, forbearance, and patience, knowing that Your kindness leads me to repentance (Romans 2:4). I confess that I have not extended the same patience and kindness to those who have hurt or offended me. Instead, I have held onto anger, bitterness, and resentment. Please bring to my mind all the people I need to forgive so that I may do so. In Jesus' name, I pray. Amen.

When we contemplate forgiveness, we often neglect two crucial parties: ourselves and God. In many cases, anger towards oneself or towards God surpasses the anger directed at any other person. Therefore, before we address the rest of the list, let us begin with forgiving ourselves and forgiving God.

The concept of letting go of anger, guilt, and self-condemnation is rooted in our failure to comprehend

God's cleansing and forgiveness. Only God can forgive our sins, which separate us from Him, and He has done so. However, we need to forgive ourselves for our failures, for letting God down, and for hurting others. Otherwise, we fall into the subtle deception that we must atone for our own sins.

Ask the Holy Spirit to reveal any areas where you need to forgive yourself and write them down:

Believers who continue to berate themselves are victims of Satan or their own distorted perception of self, rather than embracing the truth of God's grace. Forgiving ourselves grants us permission to receive God's forgiveness. It is an acknowledgment that says, "Lord, I believe that You have forgiven me and cleansed me of my sins through Your Son. Because of Your great love and grace, not because I deserve it, I choose to no longer condemn myself when You have forgiven me. I receive Your forgiveness and cleansing."

Prayer of Forgiveness for Oneself (pray this prayer aloud for each area mentioned above)

Lord Jesus, I choose to release resentment and bitterness towards myself for _____. I refuse to blame, condemn, and harbor bitterness against myself because of my past mistakes. I ask You to heal my wounded emotions. I receive the forgiveness and grace of God that covers and cleanses me from my sins. Thank You for setting me free from the bondage of bitterness and from the weight of my past experiences. In Jesus' name, I pray. Amen.

Bitterness towards God is more common than people care to admit. However, when individuals honestly confront their anger towards God, another stronghold begins to crumble. Satan's scheme is to turn us against God by planting thoughts against Him (2 Corinthians 10:4-5), leading us to rebel against His lordship. Satan is defeated when we release God from our false expectations and stop blaming Him for our own failures.

Ask the Holy Spirit to reveal any areas where you harbor bitterness towards God and write them down:

Bitterness is not always rooted in reality; it is often grounded in our perceptions. That is why it is not wrong to "forgive" God. Although God has never done anything wrong and requires no forgiveness, we must release any bitterness we hold against Him for circumstances that did not unfold as expected. As individuals work through their bitterness towards God, they quickly realize that God has never erred. Resolving bitterness towards God brings about tremendous healing and restoration.

Prayer of Forgiveness towards God (pray this prayer for each specific area mentioned above)

Lord Jesus, I choose to release resentment and bitterness towards God for _____. I renounce my right to falsely blame God, and I ask You to heal my wounded emotions. Thank You for setting me free from the bondage of bitterness and from the weight of my past experiences. In Jesus' name, I pray. Amen.

We may all be able to recall or bring to mind someone we need to forgive, but it is God who knows them all. Let us take a moment to pray and ask God to reveal to our minds those individuals we need to forgive. We must not solely rely on our memory, as we may unconsciously distort things to avoid the emotional pain attached to the event or person. So, let us pray this prayer together, seeking the guidance of the Holy Spirit.

Heavenly Father, I am grateful for the abundance of Your kindness that has led me to repentance (Romans 2:4). I confess that I have not extended that same patience and kindness towards those who have hurt or offended me. Instead, I have held onto anger, bitterness, and resentment towards them. Please bring to my mind all the people I need to forgive so that I may do so. In the name of Jesus, I pray. Amen.

As names or faces come to mind, write them down. Some may start this list with "mother, father, spouse, teachers," and so on. Others may be tempted to say, "There isn't anyone," but this is unlikely as we have all been negatively affected by someone else. God wants to liberate and set you free from this bondage, and He knows who has kept you bound, preventing you from experiencing Him fully. He has commanded you to forgive for your own sake, so He will bring to your mind both people and events that need to be forgiven.

As we embark on the journey of forgiveness, let us consider six central thoughts that underpin this transformative act:

1. Forgiveness is not about forgetting. We often hear the phrase "forgive and forget," but forgiveness is not synonymous with forgetting. Forgetting is a byproduct of forgiveness, not the means to it. When God says He "will not remember your sins" (Isaiah 43:25), He means He will not hold your past against you. Do not postpone forgiving those who have hurt you, hoping that the pain will fade away. Once you choose to forgive, Christ will bring healing. We do not heal to forgive; we forgive to heal.

2. Forgiveness is a choice. God requires us to forgive, so forgiveness is something we can do. By letting others off the hook in obedience, we break free from their control. As long as we refuse to forgive, we remain chained to our past in the bondage of bitterness. Can you imagine carrying a 5lb backpack that represents every person you have chosen not to forgive? It's time to let go.

3. Forgiveness means accepting the consequences of someone else's sin. We all live with the consequences of someone else's sin. The difference lies in whether we do so in the bondage of bitterness or the freedom of forgiveness. Jesus died as a consequence of our sins. Do not wait for the other person to ask for forgiveness. Remember that Jesus did not wait for those who crucified Him to apologize before extending His forgiveness to them (see Luke 23:34).

4. Forgiveness starts from the heart. Allow God to bring painful memories to the surface and acknowledge your feelings towards those who have hurt you. Too often, we fear the pain and

bury the emotions deep inside, pressing on with life. Forgiveness is not solely a mental action; it is a cleansing of the soul as well.

5. Forgiveness means choosing not to hold the person's sin against them. Bitter people often bring up past offenses to those who have hurt them. Misery loves company; they want the wrongdoer to suffer as much as they do. However, we must let go of the past and reject thoughts of revenge.

6. Do not wait until you feel like forgiving. Hurt from being offended often prevents us from ever "feeling" like forgiving. Make the hard choice to forgive, even if you don't feel like it. Once you choose to forgive, Satan loses his hold on you, and God will heal your damaged emotions.

Begin with the first person on your list and choose to forgive them for every painful memory that comes to mind. Stay with that individual until you are confident that you have addressed all the remembered pain. Then proceed down the list in the same manner. As you start forgiving people, God may bring painful memories to your mind that you had forgotten. Allow Him to do so, even if it hurts. God surfaces these memories so that you can confront and release them. Do not make excuses for the offender's behavior, even if it is someone close to you.

Do not say, "Lord, please help me forgive." He is already helping you and will be with you throughout the process. Do not say, "Lord, I want to forgive," as that bypasses the difficult choice we must make. Instead, say, "Lord, I choose to forgive these people and what they did to me."

For each painful memory that God reveals concerning each person on your list, pray aloud:

Lord Jesus, I choose to forgive {name the person} for {what he or she did or failed to do} because it made me feel {share the painful feelings; rejected, unloved, dirty, worthless, etc.}.

After you have forgiven every person for every painful memory, then pray as follows:

Lord Jesus, I choose not to hold onto my resentment. I release my right to seek revenge and ask You to heal my damaged emotions. Thank You for setting me free from the bondage of bitterness. I now ask You to bless those who have hurt me. In Jesus' name, I pray. Amen.

5. **Surrendering to the Lordship of Christ**

One of the greatest offenses in the Kingdom of God is rebellion. As Samuel told Saul in 1 Samuel 15:23, "Rebellion is as the divination and defiance is like wickedness and idolatry." When we rebel, we threaten the Lordship of Jesus Christ and place our own will above the commandments of God. In essence, rebellion makes us our own god.

Who do you believe is in control of your life right now? Do you think it's you? Whose voice do you primarily listen to in your decision-making? God never intended for your soul to function as its own master. Living a self-seeking, self-serving, self-justifying, self-glorifying, and self-centered life actually serves the world, the flesh, and the devil, deceiving us into thinking that we are serving ourselves (2 Timothy 3:2-5; 1 John 2:16).

Denying ourselves is the way of the Cross. Jesus reminds us that if we are to be His disciples, we must "deny ourselves, take up our crosses daily, and follow Him" (Luke 9:23). Saying "No" to ourselves and "Yes" to God is the ultimate struggle in life. However, trying to be or play God is the biggest mistake we can make. When we surrender all to God, we sacrifice the lower life to gain a higher life. Believing that the things of this world will provide us with love, joy, and peace is a lie. When you are willing to surrender to God more than to the world, you are exchanging the temporal for the eternal. It is when we allow Jesus to be Lord instead of ourselves that we open the door to a beautiful opportunity to discover the abundant resources of Heaven. Lordship is not a negative doctrine. We experience true liberation in Christ when Jesus is our Lord.

One of the main reasons we struggle to let go of our lives and place them fully under God's control is a lack of trust. We fear that if we relinquish control, God might not truly take care of us. But if we examine closely, what do we really control? The only real control we have is deciding whom we will serve. Choosing to serve God positions us to experience His faithfulness towards us (Isaiah 41:10-14).

The spirit of rebellion becomes most evident in moments of accountability to authority. We live in a rebellious age where everyone passes judgment on those in positions of authority over them. Instead of entering into the experience of worshipping God, we critique the choir at church. Rather than allowing the sermon to judge us, we sit in judgment of it. We are critical of our leaders, whether they are the president, governors, teachers, spouses, or parents. Our rebellion hinders us from practicing godly submission (Acts 6:10; 7:51).

God commands us to submit to and pray for those in authority over us (Romans 13:1-2). He desires that we yield ourselves to Him and demonstrate our allegiance by being submissive to those He has placed in authority over us. We surrender our right to rule and trust that God works through established lines of authority for our good. However, when leaders step outside their ordained function or command us to do something contrary to our commitment to the Lord, we must follow the Lord and trust that He will protect us as we honor Him (Daniel 6; Matthew 5:11-12; 6:32-33).

The word "submission" is often viewed negatively and demeaning. However, it simply means committing to follow the vision or plan of another person. Unlike some abusive leaders, God always has our best interests at heart. When we submit to His will and way, we choose to cooperate in our relationships based on God-given authority structures (1 Peter 2:13-15).

Most rebellion stems from our search for significance in a world that makes us feel insignificant. In other words, we strive to create an identity that others will consider significant in our social circles. The primary reason for this is that we are unaware of our true identity in Christ.

Take a moment to read 1 Peter 2:9. You are not just another number or random member in your community. In Christ, you are royal, chosen, holy, and special to God. You are the recipient of God's steadfast love and special compassion ("mercy").

Our position in Christ and our identity as children of God determine our significance. When our significance flows from our relationship with God, we understand that our submission to other humans does not diminish our worth. We do not need certain responses from others to gain worth. When we recognize our security in Christ, we are free to be supportive staff members and servant-leaders in the lives of others. Knowing who we are as children of God eliminates the need for rebellion, domination, and control. We yield to the Lordship of Christ, secure in our position in Him, and relate to others with love and forgiveness.

What does your act of rebellion say about your trust in God and your search for significance?

Dear Heavenly Father, You have said in the Bible that rebellion is the same thing as witchcraft and as bad as idolatry. I know that I have not always been submissive, but instead I have rebelled in my heart against You and against those You have placed in authority over me. I pray that You would show me all the ways I have been rebellious. I choose to adopt a submissive spirit and a servant's heart. In Jesus' precious name I pray. AMEN

6. Overcoming Pride and Embracing True Humility

Pride is a five-letter word with "I" in the middle. It declares, "It was my idea, and I can accomplish it through my own strength and resources." Pride is the origin of evil. As followers of Christ, we must guard ourselves against any impulses that would place our purpose, human ability, or desires at the center of our lives, causing us to neglect Jesus' Lordship and guidance in our decision-making.

Pride tells us, "I believe I can handle this on my own. It just requires hard work, human ingenuity, and perhaps a bit of luck." God says, "I won't interfere with your plan. If you want to try to save yourself, solve your own problems, or meet your own needs, you have My permission. But you won't succeed, because ultimately, you absolutely need Me, and you also need each other." Fallen humanity is like a sinking ship without God.

Pride can sneak up on even the best of us. The more we accomplish, the more susceptible we become to pride. Many Christian leaders have stumbled when they started receiving excessive praise for their work. We must be cautious not to let success "go to our heads" and set ourselves up for a fall (1 Corinthians 10:12). In short, pride can cost us everything (Proverbs 16:18).

What is humility? Humility is not saying that God is everything and we are nothing. That would be a form of false humility. Christ didn't die on the cross in vain. He was crucified to redeem fallen humanity. We are what we are by the grace of God! To deny this would discredit the work Christ accomplished on the cross. Believing that we are more than we are or that we are solely products of our own efforts aligns us with the deceived millions who have fallen victim to pride. True humility is placing our confidence where it should be. Though we have no confidence in the flesh (Philippians 3:3), we have full confidence in God and in what He can do through us. Pride says, "I did it." True humility says, "I did it by the grace of God."

People come from diverse backgrounds, but pride, rebellion, and self-sufficiency are consequences of the Fall and common to all humanity. Satan's goal is to make self-interest the chief aim of mankind. The iniquity passed on from one generation to another distorts and preoccupies us with self-will. It is the primary characteristic of false prophets and teachers (2 Peter 2:10). They operate with independent spirits and refuse to be held accountable.

Pride is the chief characteristic of the world (1 John 2:16). Though self-centeredness is the immediate evidence of pride, its root is self-exaltation. Self-exaltation, displayed through subtle attitudes of pride and self-righteousness, hinders a person from humbly admitting their need for Christ's righteousness.

A true sense of worth comes from recognizing and embracing the biblical truth that we are loved and valued by our heavenly Father. Our value is not based on our own merit, but on the fact that we are His precious children for whom Christ was willing to die (Ephesians

1:3-6). When we comprehend our worth in Christ, we no longer strive to create worth through human achievements. We can rest in the assurance that we are highly valuable to God and become the best version of ourselves by His grace through Christ.

Dear Heavenly Father, You have said that pride goes before destruction and an arrogant spirit before stumbling. I confess that I have focused on my own needs and desires and not others'. I have not always denied myself, picked up my cross daily and followed You. I have relied on my own strength and resources instead of resting in Yours. I have placed my will before Yours and centered my life around myself instead of You. I confess my pride and selfishness and pray that all ground gained in my life by the enemies of the Lord Jesus Christ would be canceled. I choose to rely upon the Holy Spirit's power and guidance so that I will do nothing from selfishness or empty conceit. With humility of mind, I choose to regard others as more important than myself. I acknowledge You as my Lord and confess that apart from You I can do nothing of lasting significance. Please examine my heart and show me the specific ways I have lived my life in pride. In the gentle and humble name of Jesus I pray. Amen

Pray through the following list and use the prayer following to confess any sins of pride that come to mind.

-Having a stronger desire to do my will than God's will
-Leaning too much on my own understanding and experience rather than God's guidance through His Word

-Relying on my own strengths and resources instead of depending on the power of the Holy Spirit

-Being more concerned about controlling others than in developing self-control

-Being too busy doing "important" and selfish things rather than seeking and doing God's will

-Finding it hard to admit when I am wrong

-Being more concerned about pleasing people than pleasing God

-Being overly concerned about getting the credit I feel I deserve

-Thinking that I am more humble, spiritual, religious or devoted than others

-Being driven to obtain recognition by attaining degrees, titles and positions

-Often feeling that my needs are more important than another person's needs

-Having feelings of inferiority appearing as false humility

-Not waiting on God

For each of the areas above that has been true in your life, pray aloud:

Lord Jesus, I agree I have been proud by (name what you checked above). Thank You for Your forgiveness. I choose to humble myself before You and others. I choose to place all my confidence in You and put no confidence in the flesh. In Jesus' name I pray. Amen

7. Breaking Free from Habitual Sin

Our lives are shaped by the habits we develop. From our daily routines to our behaviors, our lives reflect the patterns we have learned through repetition.

Unfortunately, there are areas in our lives where we may have developed habitual sins. Whether it's lying, criticizing others, or engaging in pornography, these habits go against our faith and worship. In this lesson, we will explore how to overcome these habits that are outside of God's will.

According to Charles Duhigg's book, "The Power of Habit: Why We Do What We Do in Life and Business," habits emerge as a way for the brain to save effort. The brain constantly seeks ways to turn routines into habits, as habits allow our minds to operate more efficiently. The process of habit formation occurs in a three-step loop: trigger, routine, and reward. Over time, this loop becomes automatic, with cues and rewards becoming intertwined. However, even this natural process is susceptible to Satanic sabotage. James 1:14-15 reveals that each of us has areas in which a simple cue can prompt a sinful response. Despite our commitment to Christ, we may struggle with behaviors that are deeply ingrained in our minds (Romans 7:18-21).

Nathan Azrin, a developer of habit reversal training, asserts that the brain can be reprogrammed, but it requires deliberate effort. As Paul teaches, we must intentionally renew our minds (Romans 12:2). How then can we break the cycle of habitual sin? Is confession alone sufficient? Confession involves agreeing with God and walking in the light as He is in the light (1 John 1:5-7). It is a crucial first step in repentance, but true repentance is incomplete until change is demonstrated. Confession signifies our submission to God if it is genuine and accompanied by a commitment to do His will. However, we must also resist the devil (James 4:7). Complete repentance entails submitting to God, resisting the devil, and closing the door to future temptations. The door will be fully closed when all bondages have been broken, and all mental strongholds have been dismantled. This includes renouncing the lies we have believed that contributed to our sinful behavior and choosing the truth. Transformation begins when we renew our minds with the truth of God's Word.

The Golden Rule of Habit Change is that we can't eliminate a bad habit; we can only change it. By using the same cue and providing the same reward, we can shift the routine and change the habit. Mere disgust or talk about change is insufficient. We must shift our routines from being flesh-based to being Spirit-led (Galatians 5:16-23). This requires allowing the truth of God's Word to guide our lives instead of our fleshly impulses (Psalm 119:11). Find a scripture that directs you towards a godly response rather than an ungodly one, and place it in a location easily accessible to you. Whenever you experience the cue and sense the craving, read that scripture and act upon it. When the truth of God becomes the foundation of your routine, your habits and behaviors will change (Psalm 37:31).

Overcoming habitual sin requires confessing to others (James 5:16) and to God (1 John 1:9). Simultaneously accountable to both, we must make no provision for the flesh (Romans 13:14). Developing new habits can take anywhere from 30 days to 18 months. Therefore, we must position ourselves to allow our minds to embrace the changes our spirits prompt as followers of Christ

(Ephesians 4:21-24). To begin this process, we must acknowledge the areas in need of habitual change. Let us pray this prayer together:

Dear Heavenly Father, You have instructed us to put on the Lord Jesus Christ and make no provision for the flesh and its lusts. I confess that I have given in to fleshly desires that wage war against my soul. I thank You that in Christ, my sins are already forgiven, but I have broken Your holy law and allowed sin to prevail in my body. I now come to You to confess and renounce these sins of the flesh, seeking cleansing and freedom from the bondage of sin. Please reveal to my mind all the sins of the flesh I have committed and the ways I have grieved the Holy Spirit. In Jesus' name, I pray. Amen.

Once these things have been revealed pray"

Lord Jesus, I confess that I have sinned against You by (name the sins). Thank You for Your forgiveness and cleansing. I now turn away from these expressions of sin and turn to You, Lord. Fill me with Your Holy Spirit so that I will not carry out the desires of the flesh. Amen

To complete the habitual change from sin to righteousness: Find a scripture that will prompt behavior that is in line with the Word of God and meditate upon it until it is manifested into a behavioral, mental or emotional response that glorifies God and leads to discipleship in that area.

8. Breaking Ancestral Sins

The sins of our fathers and mothers, and the resulting curses, can be a significant source of oppression in our lives. Why is this the case? It's because we, as descendants of our fathers, "take on" or "enter into" these same sins. The purpose of this study is to ensure that we understand the profound impact the behaviors of previous generations have on our lives and how our own behaviors can either perpetuate or break the cycle of sins and curses in our bloodline.

Ancestral sins represent the accumulation of all the sins committed by our ancestors. It is the inherited tendency in our hearts to rebel against God's laws and commandments, a propensity for sin that often manifests as perversion and twisted character. This accumulation of sin continues until the conditions for repentance set by God are met. The influence of these sins can be seen in various biblical references, such as Exodus 20:4-5, Deuteronomy 5:6-21, 1 Kings 16:31, 2 Kings 3:3, 10:29, and 13:2.

Unless we make intentional efforts to break free, we will perpetuate the habits, customs, and traditions passed down through generations in our families. The families we are born into and the way we are raised shape our beliefs and behaviors. Our early development, particularly our personalities, is significantly influenced by our parents. While there may be genetic predispositions, such as certain strengths and weaknesses, it is our choices that determine whether we manifest traits like alcoholism, drug addiction, or other tendencies. Moreover, our environment plays a crucial role in our development. The friends we had, the neighborhood we grew up in, the church we attended, and the influence of our parents or guardians shape us. Finally, there is a spiritual aspect to our development. God blesses those who are obedient to His covenant, while the iniquities of the disobedient are passed on to the third and fourth generations (Exodus 20:4-5).

God doesn't just see individuals; He considers how each person's life impacts and affects those who are directly connected to them, namely families. God views us as integral parts of families that have existed across generations (Deuteronomy 4:9-10).

God is both merciful and just. He is ready to forgive as soon as His conditions are met, but if those conditions are not fulfilled, His justice prevails. Consequently, the iniquities of fathers are passed down to their children, resulting in the pressure of inherited iniquity and possible curses due to their parents' sins. It is essential to appropriate the forgiveness and freedom that Jesus has provided on the cross to break the power of sin affecting us (Galatians 3:10-14, 1 John 1:9).

Taking Personal Responsibility

We will only suffer the consequences of ancestral sins if we "enter into" those same sins and make them our own. To break free, we must appropriate God's provision for freedom from sin. One way to do this is through identification repentance, which involves repenting for the sins of others. By applying the power of the cross, we can nullify the pressure of generational sins and break the power of associated curses in our lives (Colossians 2:13-14).

Experiencing freedom in Christ is an exciting journey, but it requires ongoing maintenance. While you have won a significant battle, the war continues. To maintain your freedom, it is crucial to consistently renew your mind with the truth of God's Word. Here are some practical steps to follow:

1. Remove or destroy any cult or occult objects in your home (Acts 19:18-20).
2. Get involved in a small group ministry where you can be authentic and part of a church that teaches God's truth with kindness and grace.
3. Read and meditate on God's Word daily.
4. Guard your mind, especially concerning what you watch and listen to (music, TV, etc.). Take every thought captive to obey Christ.
5. Be open and honest with God in prayer.

Our prayer is that this study has helped you connect more deeply with the truth of God's Word and experience a new level of freedom in Christ. May the Lord Jesus continue to guide your heart as you embrace the abundant life He has in store for His followers.

Ask the Lord to reveal any ancestral sins and renounce them using the following prayer:

Dear Heavenly Father, please reveal to my mind all the

sins of my ancestors that have been passed down through our family lines. As a new creation in Christ, I desire to experience freedom from these influences and walk in my new identity as Your child. In Jesus' name, I pray. Amen.

Once you have identified the ancestral sins, pray this prayer with conviction: "Lord, I renounce and confess all the family sins that You have brought to my mind. Amen."

Make the following declaration:

I hereby reject and disown all the sins of my ancestors. I have been delivered from the dominion of darkness and transferred into the kingdom of God's Son. I declare myself free from the harmful influences of ancestral sins. I am no longer defined by Adam; I am now alive in Christ. Therefore, I am a recipient of God's blessings as I choose to love and obey Him.

As one who has been crucified and raised with Christ, seated with Him in heavenly places, I renounce any and all satanic attacks and assignments directed against me and my ministry. Every curse placed on me was broken when Christ became a curse for me on the cross. I reject any claim of ownership that Satan may try to assert over me. I belong solely to the Lord Jesus Christ, who purchased me with His precious blood. I declare myself fully and eternally committed to the Lord Jesus Christ. By submitting to God's authority, I now resist the devil, and I command every spiritual enemy of the Lord Jesus

Christ to leave my presence. I put on the armor of God and stand firm against Satan's temptations, accusations, and deceptions. From this day forward, I will seek only the will of my Heavenly Father.

Conclude with the following closing prayer:

Dear Heavenly Father, I come to You as Your child, redeemed from the bondage of sin by the precious blood of the Lord Jesus Christ. You are the Lord of the universe and the Lord of my life. I offer my body to You as a living and holy sacrifice, that You may be glorified through my life and actions. I now ask You to fill me with Your Holy Spirit. I commit myself to the renewing of my mind, so that I may discern Your good, acceptable, and perfect will for me. My greatest desire is to be transformed into Your likeness. I pray and believe in the powerful name of Jesus, my Lord and Savior. Amen.

About the Author

Become the best version of you in this season so you can be what you are looking for in your relationships.

"Get Real to Get Right!"

For more resources, to follow, or information on how to book Taffiney Williams to speak at your event, please visit: or
www.facebook.com/taffineywilliams
https://www.youtube.com/@taffineywilliams
www.taffiney.com
www.amazon.com/author/taffineywilliams

Taffiney Williams is a dynamic sought after prophetic voice making waves both domestically and internationally in media and ministry. She shines in various roles, from International award winning Producer, TV host, actor, script supervisor, writer, to director. As a best-selling author, she has penned numerous impactful publications. Taffiney's ministry involves speaking engagements, conferences, mentoring, counseling, and hosting transformative virtual and in-person retreats. Her primary mission is to equip and empower individuals through her Prophetic anointing, to unleash their full potential, positively impacting the world.

Born to teenage parents, Taffiney was adopted by her great aunt and raised as an only child in Jackson, MS. From her mother's womb where she survived an attempted herbal abortion, she continues to be a testimony that God is STILL in the miracle-working business. She lives her purpose by empowering, motivating, and encouraging people to be all that God has called them to be in alignment with their purpose despite their past.

She is known as an International Speaker, Master Life Coach, Licensed Pastoral Counselor, Ordained Preacher-Teacher, Mentor, Spiritual Midwife, as well a Prophet to the Nations. With over 20yrs of ministry, she founded Journey to Impact Ministries, a team committed to helping women understand their value and identity in Christ. Through creative and innovative methods, they provide resources promoting self-evaluation leading to healing and wholeness. Her proven proprietary process delivers profound breakthrough and prophetic messages has helped leaders, coaches, visionaries, and entrepreneurs Produce in Purpose on Purpose. Taffiney Williams holds a BA from Colorado Theological Seminary. She is a sought-after Kingdom Ambassador, empowerment specialist, and transformational leader. She has earned a distinguished reputation as a catalyst of change and voice of hope. Her Kingdom Collaboration mandate has a global reach. By joining forces with partners around the world, she engages in resourcing needs that will change the trajectory of lives, legacies, relationships, and communities for generations to come.

www.ingramcontent.com/pod-product-compliance
Lightning Source LLC
Chambersburg PA
CBHW060547100426
42742CB00013B/2484